# MONEY

A CPA Exposes the Myths of

# ON

Money, Expatriation, Retirement,

# A

and Financial Predictions

# MIND

While Encouraging Happiness

## W. DURWOOD JOHNSON

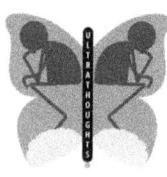

Publisher: Ultrathoughts™ LLC
ultrathoughtsbook@gmail.com
www.ultrathoughts.com

*Money on a Mind: A CPA exposes the myths of money, expatriation, retirement, and financial predictions while encouraging happiness*

Copyright © 2020 by W. Durwood Johnson.
All rights reserved. No part of this book may be used, reproduced, or transmitted in any manner whatsoever without written permission of the author.

ISBN: 9781951731069 (Print)
ISBN: 9781951731076 (Ebook)
Library of Congress Control Number: 2020901305

Cover Design by Berge Design

# CONTENTS

Preface ...................................................................................... v
Introduction ............................................................................. 1

Chapter 1: A Beautiful Delusion ......................................... 7
Chapter 2: A Reality of Money .......................................... 17
Chapter 3: Myths, a Mind Creation ................................... 31
Chapter 4: Money Myths are Simply Ideas ........................ 45
Chapter 5: Philosophically Speaking .................................. 55
Chapter 6: Society and Money Ideas .................................. 67
Chapter 7: Debt and the Imprudent Idea of Lending to God ........ 75
Chapter 8: A Myth of Being Expatriated ........................... 87
Chapter 9: Taxes and a Voluntary Myth ............................ 95
Chapter 10: The Myth of Retirement ................................. 105
Chapter 11: An Electric Prediction .................................... 119
Chapter 12: A Myth of Solvency ........................................ 123
Chapter 13: Predictions of a Mind Meant to Inspire Another ........ 133
Chapter 14: A Time to Protect and the WorthMix Model ............. 147

Conclusion: Happiness ......................................................... 163
Appendix 1: Get Ready! ....................................................... 169
Appendix 2: WorthMix Categories ...................................... 179
The Author ........................................................................... 191

# PREFACE

My life's mission is to get folks to appreciate that they create their own reality. I attempted to drive home this theme in my three-book series, *Ultrathoughts Tripartite*. In each of the brief books, it's suggested that people should think with intent and not simply be victims of the leanings of their minds. I promote the idea that we should attempt to create Ultrathoughts, deep contemplative thoughts from a mind that recognizes and attempts to suppress its innate point of view in favor of a fair-minded quest for better versions of truth.

In this book the concept is taken further; we explore the very idea of money. Throughout this book, I'm going to constantly remind you that there are no manifest truths in hopes of urging you to reconsider your current impressions about money, personal finance, and economics in general. Speaking as a financial professional having roughly thirty years' experience in the subject matter, I will expose my own money myths and offer a few predictions. With that said, like all that surrounds money and finance, these are simply ideas of a mind.

Money, and everything surrounding it, is simply that which you choose to believe. You are in charge—not politicians, economists, financial gurus, or thought leaders. You, or better said, your mind, promotes a type of illusionary reality in regard to all ideas, including money. This mental narrative, which is truly unique to you, describes your truth and urges you to continually validate existing impressions. Yes, I'm saying *it's all a delusion*.

Once you start to appreciate that there are no absolutes, you will understand that there can be no magic amount of money in your investment portfolio which brings happiness. Furthermore, no asset allocation can be proven ideal or investment return optimal. Like all others these concepts associated with money are simply myths constructed by a mind, your mind. With that being the case, if you find yourself stressed out about money or that financial success has simply passed you by, these impressions can be changed.

It's my observation that self-created money drama often saps the happiness out of life. Perhaps we should spend a bit less time chasing investment returns and significantly more time understanding how money ideas influence happiness. Once we understand ourselves, with some effort we can set prior beliefs aside and rewrite our money narrative when and how we choose. It is entirely possible that in doing so we realize that life in our modern mechanized society is far easier than we've been led to believe. We actually need very little, and just maybe it's time to reprioritize our lives once we put money ideas in their place.

# INTRODUCTION

"Get yours!" should probably be the motto of our modern society. More money earned and accumulated means you can get more stuff and/or purchase more wonderful experiences. Then what? Are you truly happier with more stuff? And, while quality experiences provide exciting material for your social media page or even the metaphorical pages of your mind, did they actually provide deep long-lasting happiness? Think about it. What if you really took time to slowly walk your dog through a park, pausing to experience every flower and every change of breeze? Couldn't that mundane experience create memories of the same quality as a similar walk through the Palace of Versailles—a trip which includes flights, hotels, and meals costing thousands? Real happiness is a product of personal judgment. Your own happiness may have absolutely nothing to do with financial success, or it could have everything to do with the value of your 401(k) account. The decision is yours alone.

Actually, money does give the appearance of having something to do with happiness. Though the research wouldn't hold up in all circumstances, it does consistently support the conclusion that some money makes people happy and a bit more than average is better still. That said, this measure of self-described happiness probably has more to do with the ease of life circumstances offered through the things which money buys. This is proven by the fact that an overabundance of money tends to make people less happy. Evidently, as life gets physically easier beyond some respectable level, there are diminishing benefits with each additional dollar. At some point, the stress of managing the money or the complexity of a life rich in stuff simply overwhelms its perceived incremental benefit. Enough is good, a bit more is better, and more still is a pain to deal with. Money is not the root of happiness.

Money is considered important to most people partially because it tends to puff the ego, resulting in personal confidence. Where did this consideration come from? Why would a notion of money seem to breed pride and confidence in people? It's a mind thing. A mind urged by society to assign importance to money is emboldened by its own success at the game of acquisition. The mind is determinative and validates the positive notions we associate with wealth and money. Money, absent contemplation, affords nothing of worth. Even the stuff money buys is meaningless, worthless—regardless of price—to one who doesn't accept the premise. Happiness can be tied to money in this same way. Money is believed to provide happiness only if one deems it to be true.

Most of us in Western society reflexively validate this narrative. More money is wonderful. Many will grant so much status to the idea that it tends to be a focal point of their lives, creating unnecessary stress and drama. Make no mistake, I value money and have my own money drama, and some of that is overtly negative. This drama is managed fairly well today, but I stop short of representing that somehow I've found the one secret to any person's true "money happiness." Mine is a premise offered which might allow you to better deal with your own issues of personal finance. It's more of a philosophy than a specific strategy. You forge your own key to resolving any issues of unhappiness with regards to personal finance. Nothing, not investment returns, the biggest home money can buy, success in your attempts to maximize the benefits of certain tax loopholes, or a massive retirement portfolio will assure true happiness.

Today, a penniless little girl in Mogadishu will have the best day of her life, while a princess in Dubai surrounded by the wealth of royalty will have her worst. The mind of one decided to choose happiness. The mind of the other likely fell into reflexive thought patterns which created an aura of negativity associated with wealth. We should each become aware of any patterns of thought which urge us toward such negative drama. In doing so, we can attempt to be an award-winning director of our own lives with intent and not simply allow innate inclination to bring about a life of angst and regret. It follows that we should respect others, allowing them to direct their own play. We're each doing our best when we elect to do something other than relying on a mind on autopilot.

Never take offense when someone thinks differently than you. This is another important aspect of my concept of creating Ultrathoughts. Society is becoming unnecessarily split along so many lines of personal preference, and some people believe they alone understand the absolute truth. They are mistaken. There is very little absolute truth in the cosmos, and ideas of money are the least of the least. Each of us is entitled to a truth provided it doesn't impose on the truth of another.

People should be concerned with properly directing their own drama in hopes of encouraging a positive tone. When your own life is harmonized, its pleasant tenor will benefit both society and the cosmos. As mutual members of a society, your happiness is important to me. We owe it to each other to seek happiness in a respectful manner.

You might be surprised to know that I'm not a professional researcher, money coach, or counselor. I haven't toured the country telling folks how to create a proper money narrative within the mind. I don't sell seminars, and I am certainly no professional author. What I am is a working certified public accountant (CPA). I'm also licensed as an insurance agent, certified financial planner (CFP®), real estate agent, and stockbroker. I spend my days immersed in issues of accounting, personal finance, general ledgers, and taxation as I manage my CPA firm located in Phoenix, Arizona. Though nothing in this book is intended to be heard as specific professional advice, I will share my thoughts based on over thirty years as a CPA and over twenty as a financial planner in hopes of informing your own money narratives. I've literally sat down with thousands of people offering personalized suggestions. Seek your own legal counsel and/or investment advice with a competent professional if you're looking for comprehensive tax or investment advice. My words are presented to inform and entertain in hopes of urging you to action—thought-action.

Most people's money drama can't be stopped entirely, but it can be better managed. We live participating in a modern mechanized society with a lot of really neat stuff. Few if any will mature to become the next Mahatma Gandhi living most of their lives without monetary wealth, simply because our very society is fueled by myths of money. These tend to dominate our relevant reality. We actually do need some money to live and participate in this modern world. Maybe this isn't right, but it is the physical existence we share in this time and space.

The point of this writing is not so much to change your mind as to awaken it to the possibility of change. Maybe it will help you appreciate that you can take steps to change your own impressions if you really wish to do so. In my years, I've come to notice several recurring themes in people's money drama, but this isn't a book about any particular script. It's a book about creating an appreciation that money itself is but a theme whose words are written within your own mind. Good or bad text, you're responsible. Your relationship with your own finances will be improved as you come to understand this script and appreciate the skill of the author—the person of you.

CHAPTER 1

# A BEAUTIFUL DELUSION

Here at the dawn of the twenty-twenties decade, the global economy is still chugging along. It's true that the economies of certain nations are struggling to keep from entering a recession, and maybe one or two are officially in one. Still, the world's economic system overall remains viable if not vibrant. This is largely because of the steadily strong purchasing power of the U.S. consumer.

This favorable economic environment for the globe has been buttressed by three important factors: a strong job market, low interest rates, and the strength of the U.S. dollar. Combine these factors with a strong housing market and record stock market performance, and people will remain in the mood to spend. It's quite possible that these favorable characteristics will continue for years to come. After all, the best predictor of tomorrow is what happens this evening. This has always been the case, and this force of inertia might just continue for some extended period of time. Still, every now and then inertia is overcome. An unexpected paradigm shift or systemic change ushers in a fresh trend.

We may be in the midst of a shift today: a paradigm shift that brings forth a better world. The beautiful delusion of many is that technology, not the least of which is fifth-generation ultra-highspeed wireless communication (5G), will literally change our lives for the better within a decade. Just imagine seamless connectivity to all the information in the world in any physical location you occupy at the moment. You'll soon be able to walk into a room that autonomously senses your desires and customizes your experiences to your liking. If you prefer a certain type of music, when you open the door your favorite genre will be playing. If you like sports, your room will literally be decorated via holographic display in the colors and logos of your favorite team. You won't need to change a channel, search through news you don't like to read in order to see news you do, or request much of anything. Artificial intelligence (AI) enabled devices will preemptively anticipate your desires by calculating the odds that you prefer this over that, and then simply make a decision calculated to optimize your physical experience.

Have you ever had a really bad experience at a movie, on a cruise, or even at that cool restaurant your friends raved about? Your great-great-great-grandchild may not. AI could predict what she will like and just might not dare fill her environment with offensive experiences.

AI will customize our immersive personal experience much sooner than most can comprehend. Within a decade or so, many of us won't encounter negative experiences unless we choose to do so. Our self-created world will be continually affirmed via predictive technology. Just think about it—we'd never hear awful music because our personalized experience culls these unpleasantries before we encounter them. Positivity may be the only experience of our relatives five to ten generations from now. Maybe sooner.

As time passes, many if not most humans will come to view the world as a kind of "me world." Obviously, there is not one "me" on the planet. Each individual comes to view truth and reality as agreeable to their ways of living and thinking. We come to believe this reality of self is a shared truth, and within a circle of like-minded thinkers, it can be. However, make no mistake. Your truth will never be one hundred percent my own. Every single person, deep within, cherishes their own set of alternative facts.

The actual physical experience of living itself will be improved within twenty years. Think about having personalized medical attention which is literally designed around your genome. You will be maintained to be as healthy and durable as any physical organism can be tuned through nutrition, coaching, and pharmaceuticals. You will live as vibrant a physical life as our species has ever lived in its 250,000 years on this planet.

Finally, pause and let this prediction sink in. Within a hundred years or so it may be possible that human beings aren't actually required to know anything. Forget education; that will be considered an absolute waste of time unless the experience is sought for mere entertainment. All that can be known at any moment will simply be there, within the ether. This will be the world that our great-great-great-grandchildren will be born into. Most of us have little appreciation for what is about to happen on this planet. Didn't modern humans stop rubbing sticks together in order to start a fire once they had a lighter in their pockets? I suppose some still choose to rub those sticks, but really, what's the point? Innovation transfers self-reliance to systems and machines. Absent some unforeseen event, the "good life" for humans is about to get a whole lot better.

For all of this good stuff to happen, basically all we need to do is not screw things up too badly. We can't decide to completely ruin our environment, start a massive nuclear war, or set off a regional electromagnetic pulse weapon. Historically speaking, life's pretty darn good today and will be far better in the next decade. Sure, occasionally some nutjob goes off the rails, but keeping the history of humanity in perspective, we're in very good shape. Just maybe life will stay this way for a thousand years, benefiting billions more. After all, once a system as massive and complex as the global economy starts clicking on all cylinders, this positive rhythm tends to continue until something big happens.

As time passes there becomes a dynamic synergy between a system and its participants. They sort of feed upon each other. The global economy is among the biggest, most complex, and dynamic systems ever created by our species. When it's moving in one direction or another it is extremely difficult to change its momentum. Spending is assumed to be the primary manner that participants express their optimism regarding their personal finances. With their credit cards and mobile pay devices in hand, shoppers seem to be willing to carry debt like never before. Optimism helps to keep shoppers shopping, companies making money, and investors buying investment assets. The global economy is doing really well. Positive people impact the economy in positive ways.

Besides the consumers being in a good mood, we can't deny that governments seem to be acting with a smile on their proverbial faces. Sovereign governments are willing to take on more debt than ever before. Sure, they need to print money to do so, but across the globe, governments in charge of the world's leading economies seem to be able to print money which ends up finding a productive use. Though we don't quite know for sure whether it's foolishness or confidence which is driving their actions, it's apparent that economic leaders believe our global economy has the ability to use massive amounts of new currency printed. Unless or until the global economic system rejects the influx of new money, governments will continue to create more and more new fiat currency. The circumstance of printing new money, and new debt created by association, will probably continue for many more years to come.

On the other hand, maybe the delusion described is a bit too pretty. All of this positivity is fine and well, but aren't there some troubling signs? Possibly you have noticed how divided our society has become. That's probably not good for society or business. Might that be a precursor to some fundamental problems? For one, this whole national or global debt thing seems to have really gotten out of hand. The figures are nearly unfathomable. Isn't a stack of a trillion one-dollar bills something like 67,866 miles high? And isn't the debt of the United States government $22 trillion? Oh, and is anybody ever going to fix our health insurance model? My goodness, funding the cost of family health insurance today is the equivalent cost of buying a new car, burning it to ash in December, and then repurchasing it in January. If some leader or some congress doesn't address these problems, wouldn't that prevent us from obtaining the incredibly wonderful future that seems to be within our grasp?

It's rather natural for people to fear the unknown, and in my own mind-myth, these are some major unknowns. Being a person who rather lives the world of money, frankly, I'm a bit fearful about our economic future in the near term. If my instincts prove prophetic and economic hard times do hit within the next ten years or so, those of us with retirement in mind within the next decade are likely to be in a world of hurt. If financial disaster hits the U.S., most of us in our fifties and sixties don't have enough high-earning years left in employment to earn back what we'd likely lose in a major financial recession. The last recession saw housing prices fall by 60% and the broad stock market drop by roughly 50%. Sure, each has recovered, but that recovery probably wouldn't have happened without unprecedented measures by the government. Would unprecedented measures save us again? Assuming the next recession is as bad as the last, if not worse, try to imagine watching your investment asset values decline by 60%, 70%, or more—and then not recovering their values within your lifetime.

There are an awful lot of *ifs* in my words. Global dynamics and the U.S. economy are unpredictable. We can think something will happen, but in a sense, it really doesn't mean much. We know nothing about the future and can merely guess. My delusion can be beautiful or a nightmare; either way, it's simply an opinion—guesses within a delusion created in my mind.

So what's the point of thinking or guessing if we won't be correct anyway? After all, our very existence is but a script which is only revealed with every passing breath of life. I can't somehow breathe faster and take a quick look ahead with certainty in mind. Guessing, or more specifically predicting, is what the brain and its product the mind do. We are creatures who exist in partnership with a predictive machine. It is through hopeful anticipation of the words of the next chapter that we live a happy existence on this planet. Unknowns tend to make many of us uneasy, so we seek to resolve our questions by making guesses to ease the mind. Fair-minded guesses are preferred to those which are reflexive and ill-informed.

I prefer to stay positive, so I'd rather train my mind to hope for a healthy and happy ninetieth birthday than one that will face some challenges. With that said, I am who I am: a very pragmatic and logically-oriented person. I can't simply wake up, read a few self-scribed positive affirmation notes, and become a person who truly lives life as it comes. Living through my own happy ninetieth birthday is not as likely as never living to see the year. I know this for sure, and I can't simply ignore the fact that very few people see their own ninetieth birthday.

When it comes to my personal finances, I wish to stay optimistic. However, I can't maintain such spirit without a fair-minded appreciation of the risks. Things happen in life which derail the best-laid plans for financial success. Some of those events are truly unpredictable and any attempt to plan for them would be utterly meaningless, while others can be anticipated. Selling a million copies of this book is as unlikely as me winning a multimillion-dollar lottery, so I won't quit my day job in anticipation of either. However, though I don't think I'm at grave risk for a stroke, it's certainly possible given my family history. So it would be prudent to purchase long-term care insurance.

For me to maintain some sense of optimism that I will live to see ninety, I shall act as if I will. This opinion, an idea, informs me that I need to save money for a future period when I won't be physically able to earn a living. Saving syncs up with my desire to be optimistic about my own longevity. Conversely, if I never saved for old age, I am by implication denying the very possibility within my own myth. When I choose to act in ways that respect my mind and have a positive spin, I am reconciling the tone of my actions to that of my mind. I am a pragmatist who is a planner at heart, or better said, a left-brain oriented person who has a compelling desire to prepare. When I don't prepare, this gives me anxiety and stress.

We must never deny the power of the mind. If a mind simply thinks it's wise to be cautious, that mind must be cautious to be content. You can't train an eager beaver to be a laid-back hound dog any more than you can convince your hypochondriac best friend that the discolored place on her neck is probably just a mole. If, within my mind, I've decided that troubling economic times are in my near future, there is little doubt that I would personally have feelings of regret, stupidity, and possibly even depression if I failed to act in harmony with my thoughts. It is rather obvious that my mind is the driver of my personal happiness. I can take steps to act happier, and possibly I can even influence myself to be somewhat more laid-back, but if deep within my mind I don't buy into the premise, I will never actually obtain happiness. The deep thoughts of my mind are in control.

A person who for whatever reason thinks as they do is best served by acting in harmony with their own thoughts and opinions—experts be damned. If one believes caution and protective actions should be taken, to deny this instinct will create unhappiness. Obviously, the converse is true as well. If one prefers to never plan, even for the most likely of events, that's fine as well. Live a life that acknowledges the way you think and the person you are without fear. If either approach, planning or not, is ultimately proven to have been the absolutely wrong action, yes, there will be regret. However, this emotion will be temporary for the simple fact that it was merely a failure in judgment, not a failure that disrespects the self.

Happiness is derived contextually; therefore, true happiness reconciles actions with one's own values and beliefs. For this reason, one should strive to understand the self and attempt to pin well-conceived ideas to their internal narrative. This book promotes my belief that enlightened views may be sought in regard to all ideas—even those as urbane as money.

Continually ask yourself questions as you contemplate the influence of money on your life. Explore your mind and maybe even invalidate your prior beliefs in hopes of refreshing more lucid views of money and personal finance. Once you've admitted the way you've historically viewed money and come to appreciate certain myths surrounding its idea within your own mind, you can isolate these beliefs and reconsider their worthiness.

That reconsideration shall be from a mind that recognizes its bias inclination and suppresses its influence on further judgments through ultra-thinking. These Ultrathoughts are still your delusion, but they are forever beautified for the simple fact that they are intentional thoughts. They represent the best ideas you can conceive. After their creation, you might find that you've reprioritized certain aspects of your own life ... including your ideas of money and personal finance.

CHAPTER 2

# A REALITY OF MONEY

This book is a product of my mind, not scholarly analysis or predictive analytics. Maybe it should rest on a philosophy shelf rather than one on personal finance. Not that I don't respect analysis typically associated with finance, but to tell you the truth, I don't actually put much faith in scientific methodology when it comes to predicting issues related to economics. Financial experts are wrong far more often than they are correct, and economists are even worse at predicting than *The Old Farmer's Almanac*. Frankly, I don't know why we consider economists anything other than soothsayers. Given that comment, you'd probably be surprised to learn that some of my favorite books and podcasts are about the economy. However, I take their words as philosophy. Theirs are simply opinions expressed, not manifest facts.

What I do put faith in is my overarching premise of the benefits of ultra-thinking. I assume fair-minded contemplation is better than not. This book was written based on my best attempts to respect my premise. I'm going to tell you what I think and give you nothing other than my word that I have derived fair-minded conclusions from a mind that has attempted to restrain its innate bias. This bias is inborn in each of us and tints all judgment to one degree or another. It probably can't be overcome, but it can be restrained with intent, and when it is, an Ultrathought is possible. Furthermore, I suggest that it is far more important that you appreciate what you think than simply accept my own conclusions. This coming decade, the twenty-twenties, will present a number of challenges for people in the United States; of that I am as certain as one can be. Yes, it's still a delusion, but I own it.

If you're familiar with my earlier books, you know that I promote a particular type of purposeful thinking. Ultra-thinking is a term I use to describe deep contemplative thought accomplished while restraining your predisposition to think a certain way. Naturally, I am not the perfect practitioner of my own premise, but I try rather consistently. Underpinning this principle are two key facets:

We all are biased to one degree or another.

Reality is a perception of your mind; a mere delusion.

These two facets often elicit a visceral response. I've been blasted on multiple occasions for daring to suggest a client or family member is biased. It's probably because I make a definitive statement, not a suggestion. I specifically state that we are all biased to one degree or another, period. Some folks find such a proclamation not only offensive but arrogant and unfair. "You don't know me!" is a rather consistent outburst. Respectfully, I ask them to consider the second facet before storming off: It's all a self-created delusion anyway.

Acceptance of the second premise before the first will often help put them at ease when I dare proclaim that their current position is biased absent ultra-thinking. Once people can appreciate that all that is relevant in their whole existence just might be a bundle of mental interpretations, they can often start to recognize the futility of angry disagreement. My statements—whether they're on finance, economics, politics, childrearing, or the Godhead—are mere opinions and are not a threat to your own. Yes, we are all biased, including me. Therefore, if we disagree, we do so through our own unique type of dogmatic fog of interpretation. If you want to believe confidence in my premise makes me arrogant, I'm fine with that. However, make no mistake, I am not unfair. I am immersed within my own fog of delusion, but I do at least attempt to notice its stench.

I assume we are each doing the best we can within our own delusion. For reasons only known by the Godhead, we are each individually special creatures on this planet. I can accept your own vehement disagreement with me on this point. I truly don't care what you think about God or the spiritual realm. I can even accept a pure ideologue, though they typically have no respect for me. I simply request that such a person admit their mind is made up, and given they have a right to their opinion, I have a right to my own. It's all a delusion anyway.

Success in ultra-thinking will produce an Ultrathought. These are fair-minded thoughts assumed superior for the simple fact that they are derived from an earnest attempt to push the mind to its limits while attempting to restrain the influence of personal dogma and presupposition. An ultra-thinker seeks clarity and has no need to promote self, ideology, or social agenda. They can express confidence in that which they have contemplated but stop short of demanding universal agreement. They readily accept that their mind may one day change, though, like any other person, an ultra-thinker may fervently believe they are right. Of course, they are still wrong from the view of one who disagrees. Regardless, they are undeterred. They don't need to answer the questions of humanity, simply the questions of their own mind. Ultra-thinkers have a thirst for optimal ideas in the satisfaction of self.

Once the optimal is obtained, they feel a certain degree of comfort simply because they believe they've figured "it" out. They often experience a feeling of enlightenment, yet in the back of their mind, they understand true enlightenment is unobtainable. Nevertheless, they will always continue the journey once the mind comes to recognize both the beauty and futility of thought. Like a favorite melody or a beautiful sunset, a truly perfect Ultrathought never exists. The real joy is in the seeking, not the knowing.

Seeking your own optimal ideas associated with money might strike you as a rather odd philosophical journey to undertake. On the contrary, it is probably one of the best. Money is so integral to our lives today that I'm hard-pressed to understand why more people don't delve deep into their own money drama and try to figure things out. Money is both the fuel for our modern mechanized society and the theory which grounds our economic system. There isn't a person involved in our society who doesn't engage their mind's money impressions dozens if not hundreds of times each day.

I'm not saying it's right or wrong, but I do believe people think more on a daily basis about money than they do their God, life's purpose, personal health, or the environment. They almost have to in order to function in society. Who doesn't make or ponder a purchase? Goods and services don't simply arrive like they did when we were eight years old.

As a working adult, in any given year you spend more or less 50% of your time dealing with work-related activities. That time not only includes your actual working hours but the hours associated with commuting, education, and preparation. Now, I'm assuming you don't work for free; therefore, though it may not be your only reason for working, a substantial reason for working is the acquisition of money.

People do what they want to do absent bondage. All obligations are in fact a mere acquiescence to your own willful mind. You won't walk unless your mind agrees, and you won't work unless you choose to do so. We choose to work because our mind believes we should or must. Like getting out of bed, work won't happen unless you decide to do the act. Work is a belief, a delusion adopted.

We aren't slaves to work; we are creatures who bow to the master of our mind. So when we complain about work and those complaints continue for months on end, it has always been my view that some self-reflection should be done. Contemplate the circumstance elected. Either find a different job or admit that your complaints are a self-serving diatribe with a purpose. Now I'm not saying that purpose is wrong. I'm simply stating the obvious. Complaining about work for some is more of a strategy to get more *from* work, including sympathy, than it is an attempt to get more money. The value of work received by the worker is increased through an attachment of "sympathy" to any tangible dollars earned.

The mind is your boss, not the individual who manages your working hours. The mind is its own master, but it can be directed by the person it created, the person of you. I direct my mind that work is what I want to do and that I will be happier as a result. In my mind, each is of significant value. My personal narrative is written this way. Others will have a different narrative. Possibly they don't value either happiness or work. To each their own.

Having deluded myself as to the value of work and its result, money, I can justify a significant allocation of my time on earth in pursuit of money. I've harmonized the entire equation: mind, work, money, physical effort, mental effort, and my person. Like many people, I obtain a sense of fulfillment from my work. This fulfillment includes both a validation of self and the very real stuff of U.S. dollars in my wallet. Therefore, we could say that though I accept I'm not required to work, I shall continue to work because I have internalized two basic truths. First, I like my career and feel emotionally better by speaking with people who I believe appreciate what I do. Second, I like money and the experiences and things it buys. At the point one of these reasons is no longer validated within my mind, I won't choose to work. These are my work-related myths which are intertwined with my beliefs about money and compensation.

Most of us start working at a young age because we are influenced by society to believe we should. We might even be told by parents or peers that we must work for a variety of very specific reasons. As people mature, some come to believe they must work for a lifetime. Others have literally never worked a day in their lives. Our ideas about work which tend to be tied to our money myths start subconsciously at a very young age.

The idea that one absolutely must work is not part of my own delusion; however, it was prior to my own ultra-thinking of the subject. I simply assumed, reflexively, that an able-bodied citizen must work and never deeply contemplated the question. At a very young age, I started to reason that it was a kind of moral failure not to work. Like many in Western society, I believed a "good" job is a worthy goal and such a job should pay a "fair" wage. Quotations are used to denote these terms are highly subjective.

The idea that to work a good job means one shall receive a fair wage urged me toward assumptions about the state of those I met. As a young man, I reflexively assumed that the amount of money one earned was directly tied to their effort. Absent the occasional lottery winner, criminal score, or heiress windfall, I assumed pretty much everyone was adequately rewarded for their effort. This, of course, is a documented fallacy, but it was my personal truth for decades. Why? I never really thought about it. I was a reflexive left-brainer too busy working to obtain my own just rewards and rather casually adopted beliefs promoted by my community.

As time passed, what was obvious to so many of you became somewhat evident to me. Life, our wins and failures, and certainly one's own stack of available money is not doled out fairly. I literally had to ultra-think this very question: the unfairness of earnings with respect to one's effort. I had to unlearn or rewrite my mind-myth in order to accept the idea that life is not fair, and certainly the money one earns is not exclusively tied to their own efforts. Yes, I've since determined, the person digging a ditch should earn more than the CPA, the president of the largest bank in town, the baseball pitcher, or the actor simply because that ditchdigger expends more overall effort. I make this proclamation respecting a professional baseball player spends years perfecting a skill and a CPA studied really hard to pass an exam. To the point, I remind you baseball is a game and studying for an exam is typically done sitting on a pretty darn comfortable chair.

Life is not fair, so the laborer who works a lifetime is not paid a fair wage but a wage that society has somehow determined. It is societal opinion that effectively determines compensation, not one's boss or employer, and it is luck that determines whether the wishes of society are granted. In the U.S., our society has determined a major league baseball pitcher, a rare commodity, is more valuable than a hundred ditchdiggers. Is it fair? No. Is it equitable? Probably—given our societal values. Of course, societal values are certainly not global. Who is more valuable in the jungles of Bangladesh? Wouldn't one really good ditchdigger be worth a whole bunch of National League pitchers?

A recognition of the unfairness of the distribution of our "rewards" of the physical world (tangible money, physical pain, material stuff) has not made me angry or even negative. In fact, it has made me somewhat sanguine. Hopefully this confidence won't be taken as arrogance, but here it goes. Attempting to win the game of life by thinking you can righteously accumulate treasure is, in my view, a rather ill-conceived delusion. Money is not a just reward. It's useful, and in some cases it takes on the appearance of being fairly allocated, but in the end there are no just physical rewards, only a righteous engagement of the game we call our own physical existence.

Having applied my ultra-thinking premise to the idea of money, I can now appreciate that the person sleeping on the sidewalk without a job is not automatically a person of flawed moral character. I don't know these people and certainly am not wise enough to judge their character. It's possible that some people don't even want to work. That doesn't make these folks wrong. If we all thought that way (not wanting to work), that would be a problem for a society that relies on commerce, but we don't. So let them sleep provided they're not breaking some law.

My default assumption is that humans are kind people and tend to act as such. When our health is good and the mind is clear we usually act in ways that put the odds in our favor. Those odds include that if you get a good education and get a good job, you'll likely earn enough money to purchase the stuff you believe you need to survive adequately in the modern world. Assuming one wishes to participate in our society, as most do, this money myth to which we subscribe seems to work well enough. Still, we must admit sometimes the odds playout as expected, other times not. Major facets related to the money game don't follow any rules and certainly ignore the odds. An automobile accident, an unexpected heart attack, or the birth of a handicapped child, and just maybe you lose the money game despite playing the odds to perfection.

Money, as a physical thing in our hands, is the result of any number of events. Stay healthy, perform a service that society values or simply get lucky, and you'll have money. Some of these results make sense in my reality, others not so much. Regardless, the fact that I can't make sense of why a person does or doesn't have money is as irrelevant as the color of their shoes. Money as compensation, payment, or prize often has nothing to do with a person's character, effort, or morality. Eventually, I came to understand that to assume it always does is a devaluation of the very concept of morality itself.

Like so many of my quests to figure things out, my money journey was not elected. I was perfectly happy for the first fifteen or twenty years in my career. I had no burning desire to rewrite let alone destroy my own money narrative. Remember I am an accountant, so I've historically walked around in a very dense fog of money dogma. Like an electrician, educator, doctor, or any other career professional, I didn't desire to shred that chapter of my personal narrative titled "All I know about my job." Still, once I began to ultra-think various big topics, reality, and the Godhead, they started to bleed over into more mundane matters. I started questioning any number of subjects: global warming, the death penalty, vegetarianism, and then the tone and texture of my money myths. It became clear that money was a different kind of idea. An idea with incredible depth in society and influence on my life. Money really seems to be a weird kind of demigod who dominates American society. My impression of its very nature is tied up into my impressions of all kinds of notions. For example:

- How hard someone works and for how much

- Should I sell my home or put on that addition?

- Why I pay taxes and others don't

- Am I working for the love of money, my wife, my retirement, or my life?

- What is my own economic future?

As an American in his late fifties, I'm particularly concerned about the final question: my economic future. I suspect in my life I've spent thousands of hours pondering and indeed ultra-thinking the issue. In contemplation of this very broad question, I've drawn some conclusions—dare I say Ultrathoughts—about how things are likely to play out in the coming decade. These represent a sample of my own money myths and though they may be proven wrong in time, they are my truth today.

Certainly, the final mass of baby boomers in the United States will be retiring from full-time employment en masse. One would assume the gross domestic product (GDP) of certain individual states will decline for several years in a row. And it's entirely possible that the ripple effects of this coming economic downturn will not only impact my personal wealth but tax collections. One would assume this would place tremendous pressure on the government to provide services and even fund my all-important social security pension payment.

This group of citizens, boomers, will be attempting to divest from certain investment classes, not the least of which is their home. All within a period of five to fifteen years a substantial percentage of boomers will sell single-family homes which are primarily located in the suburbs. Most hope to receive fair prices if not top-dollar when they sell. Most had banked on converting home equity into ready cash. Unfortunately, there won't be enough Generation X (those born within the two decades following the boomers) buyers willing to pay fair dollar, and the millennial age cohort (those born in the 1980s through the later '90s) is somewhat "stuff" averse. Very soon there will be a crash in single-family home values, and the worst segment of real estate will be mini mansion or move-up homes. There will be no noticeable bounce back or recovery after the crash in many markets, particularly those of the suburbs.

The retirement portfolios of Americans are traditionally weighted toward publicly traded common stocks. This has been the case since the popular rise of investment accounts known as 401(k)s and Individual Retirement Accounts (IRAs). While this has been good for investors holding these stocks and pools of stocks, known as stock mutual funds, these investments will need to be sold to generate cash. Stock investments will be liquidated en masse, releasing an unprecedented amount of value. Unlike homes, individual stocks are sold on an auction market. As long as the market is open a buyer will generally be found at whatever price. What this means is that when an investor offers a stock for absolute sale, that sale occurs in an auction environment. It is entirely possible that this dynamic—massive quantities of stock being liquidated—will result in huge investment losses for boomers.

Boomers, like any investor, must ultimately absorb any loss the best they can. Retired folks can't always wait for the best price or even a fair price; they must continue to spend on food, housing, and, of course, healthcare. In this fire-sale environment created by the boomers, neither Generation X nor millennial citizens have anywhere near the amount of accumulated net worth to pick up the slack in the housing, bond, or stock markets. Every single investment class of assets will experience selling pressure, and though some investments will fare worse than others, it is literally impossible to predict the ultimate biggest loser.

Though it could take thirty years for all of this to play out, I suspect it will become obvious that there is a problem within a decade. Once the problem becomes known it is entirely possible that all hell will break loose rather quickly. There could be a race to exit investments, and more folks will get hurt than get out. To play defense one must assume all investment classes will be trashed to the point of utter ruin. Us common folk will be competing with the world's largest banks to get through this exit door, so I'd rather be early than a member of the hoard. I'm willing to get defensive now rather than hope to squeeze a bit more return. The world is awash in cash and debt. The financial bigwigs aren't going to save common folk like you or me. If they can save anybody, which is doubtful, it will be themselves just as it has been so many times before.

No country, no currency, or economic model lasts for an eternity. Furthermore, capitalism, the foundation of our global economy, requires a cost of capital (positive rates) to function. When significant amounts of debt are created using negative rates, that means the system isn't functioning. In my view, the world is ripe for a very big change for a variety of reasons, but it will be the mass of retiring boomers in the United States which ultimately pushes the system too far. Therefore, the only question is when, not if. Since most of us boomers will only be alive another twenty or thirty years at best, the way I figure, there's far more upside to reasonable preparation than downside. It's time to get financially defensive.

I simply can't afford to lose 70–90% of my net worth and still be financially settled in my old age. And, yes, that's how bad I believe it will get. The values of certain very popular investments and possibly entire investment classes will be decimated, in my opinion. Once values are adjusted downward, many investment assets will not recover their value during my lifetime.

CHAPTER 3

# MYTHS, A MIND CREATION

While reading this short book, pause from time to time. Really try to understand yourself and gauge your own beliefs about money and personal finance. Be fearless as you contemplate in hopes of gaining a deeper understanding of self. Don't fear my words about the economy or those of anyone else. Ours are simply opinions based on internal themes self-constructed within a mind. I am telling you *the experts literally know nothing*. They can't accurately predict the way the system will react when they don't even know the variables!

You should be more inspired to ultra-think your own personal financial situation because you alone will suffer the consequences. I believe several things are likely to occur with regard to the global economy and strategize my own personal finances accordingly. I'm going to tell you how I see things, but ultimately, it is your view which matters. With due respect, though, I suggest you should protect what wealth you've created. I personally believe you should concentrate more on peace of mind than getting a bigger piece of the pie. Your personal happiness is improved when you take steps to understand money and finance simply because they play such a huge role in your life here in our modern mechanized society.

Continuing along that same line of thought, I believe that people are more likely to be happy when they recognize that they have created their person. If they are unhappy with that being, change. Such a change can occur, but it will always take effort. Life's fleeting, and the life you live is based on your actions, whether those actions are intentional or reflexive.

The life you live manifests your truth and reality, not mine. True, we share a particular physical existence dictated largely by the earth and our sun. We interact this day within a common time and space. We as a species seem to share some basic understanding with regards to right and wrong. It appears we humans want to cooperate even as we individually seek our own happiness. Personally, I am more settled being around cooperative happy people and assume you feel the same.

That said, we aren't all alike, and certainly as we age differences in our worldviews become apparent. Some of us, left-brainers, prefer to assume the universe and life in general is rather well structured and rational. Others, right-brainers, are most comfortable in a reality that is fundamentally balanced and egalitarian. I am not saying the mind of either a more rational person or more egalitarian is superior. Just the opposite. Each is superior from the perspective of the owner of their position. In turn, each view is inferior from the eyes of the observer. Few are so extreme as to be unequivocally characterized as being wholly driven by either their left or right. Nevertheless, we each lean to an extent, and that lean tends to become more pronounced if it matures in an environment that never challenges the orientation. We grow to think a particular way, and absent intent to think beyond inclination, some will become so immersed in their self-created view of the world they can scarcely understand the perspective of those who fundamentally think differently.

Societies and regional cultures also tend to express a tone to their perspective. It's no mystery that folks from Beijing, China, have a different perspective on life than people in Dallas, Texas. Neither culture owns a view which is manifestly better or worse, but members of these societies perceive the world somewhat differently. Consider how each society tends to assess their own sons and daughters.

People in the United States certainly love their children unequivocally. Though individually we may prefer one gender of child to another, our reality is one of little real preference of gender. Our friends in China undoubtedly love their children every bit as much as we do. Parent-child bonds aren't cultural; they're a genetic trait of our species. Still, we need to be honest.

Most parents on mainland China treat and indeed cherish a male child more than a female child. This is a cultural difference between the United States and China. It's quite apparent to anyone who knows the culture that, on the whole, the Chinese take more personal pride in the accomplishments of a son than a daughter. There are various reasons for this which are beyond this discussion; nevertheless, I stand by my assertion. This is their truth.

Here in the U.S., we're far less apt to make such an overt distinction. Since roughly the 1970s there has been an overt trend wherein women and men are equally valued. That movement has helped change family and childrearing dynamics. Boys and girls within a family in the U.S. are more or less equally valued by their parents. This is not the case in China. What this means is that the "truth" or "reality" of citizens in these two different countries is different.

Does that literally mean a male firstborn is actually "better" than a daughter in China simply because that's the perspective of the average Chinese citizen? Who would ever say such a son is superior to a daughter? Oh, I know—about a billion and a half Chinese folks! So, in the interest of expanding our perspective and better appreciating how one's mind drives their own truth, let's have an open, honest, and fair-minded discussion.

Naturally, we must recognize that one's simple opinion does no harm to another, and my discussion of a society doesn't mean I in any way endorse their beliefs. I cannot change the average Chinese citizen any more than I can change the weather. As ultra-thinkers, we shall freely observe and seriously ponder the outrageous. When attempting to ultra-think, you may want to pretend you're in a philosophy class with the doors locked and all the smartphones sequestered. There are no awkward statements in a room of true philosophers. Now let's take a deep breath and truly dive deep to contemplate this question while suppressing our outrage.

If, in the minds of the parents, all of the hopes and dreams of a noble Chinese family are tied up in the birth of a firstborn son of the Zhang family living in southeastern Beijing, wouldn't that then actually mean this male child is indeed more important to the Zhang parents than your own child is to you? Pause and ponder the issue for a moment, and you'll glean some insight into how you think. Consider this issue from a fair mind that has suppressed its predisposition to be offended by ideas that run counter to its historical version of truth.

It's your perspective that guides your own truth. Your life, your reality, is a product of your self-created mind myth. That book of the mind is your story. As time passes and you encounter new situations, you insert pages within this personal narrative. Very rarely would you intentionally shred a chapter from your book and start anew. As U.S. citizens, we're not inclined to give respectful consideration that it could be true that sons are actually more important than our daughters. For most in the U.S., our personal narratives are in agreement and are written in a definitive manner with regards to this idea: the sexes are equal. This is our shared settled fact.

The average Chinese person doesn't write this chapter as we do because they are evil or misguided. They write as they do because this is their reality. It fits nicely within their own historical set of truths. These truths have been internalized, and neither we nor they will have a change of mind unless we first open our minds to serious and fair-minded contemplation. Earnest ultra-thinking might lead to a change of heart, or not. Everyone has a unique truth, a unique version of the enlightenment they have found.

Pushing my premise further, I'll risk angering you more. Our friend in China, Mr. Zhang, is entitled to his truth. In his defense, we must appreciate that societies express values that are forced on their members either casually or overtly. Eventually, I'd assume that Chinese society will express a different version of truth—a truth like our own—but for now the Chinese have their reality and we have ours. As far as I know, Mr. Zhang hasn't harmed his children or our very humanity simply because he favors one gender over another. In fact, I'll remind you that as a parent we all screw up our kids. It's just a question of how we do it. This father loves his children, and I assume he's an asset to our world. Though I would urge him to ultra-think the issue of sexism within his narrative in hope of urging him toward enlightenment, I will say, "Let this parent have his truth."

We can recognize the unfairness of discrimination based on the gender of a child because we live where we do. We can seek to influence the world to believe as we, and I'm within my rights to criticize his view. Still, Mr. Zhang is not manifestly wrong. He is correct within the context of his society in his given time and space.

The use of a rather sexist parent in an attempt to have you appreciate that we each individually have a reality that is bolstered by our peers might strike you as odd. However, by getting you just a bit angry, maybe I've expressed my point. We can share some views, sometimes, but ultimately we won't agree on every single truth. You like your politicians, I like mine. I have my spin on life, you have yours. We tend to think of things a certain way because of our history and brain leaning toward left or right. Among those "things" are unique perceptions about money, wealth, retirement, finance, etc. We each have a reality that is foundational to the person we become.

It may be time to rethink your historical truth about money because you've probably been misled by both society and your patterns of thought. These "less than optimal" ideas may be negatively influencing your life. Frankly, you are running out of time, and I do mean this literally. We are in for some tough times fiscally, and you should get yourself ready. Just maybe you've fallen into reflexive patterns of thought with regards to finance which are creating unnecessary stress and anxiety. Dare to rewrite a few pages, or even remove a chapter from your own mind-myth narrative.

Before you start rewriting or even shredding your historical money narrative, maybe you'd best start with getting a better understanding of the person you've created. How do you lean? Do you tend to rather casually assume life is fair and that somehow you'll be okay—financially-oriented toward thoughts of the right brain hemisphere? Or, are you so logical that you've created multiple formulas that measure and anticipate every move of the U.S. stock market—oriented toward the left side of the brain?

Neither style of thinking about money is wrong; however, each and every person can be better by guarding against their own tendency to think reflexively. Reflexive thought is often rooted in core beliefs which are not particularly well conceived.

That fundamental outlook, your mind-myth, impacts how you view the world and guides your interpretations of the reality that presents itself before you.

Mind-myth is a somewhat common way to characterize your internal story or narrative. The word *myth* in this context simply infers that we create a set of beliefs. This in no way indicates either the myth or its creation is in any way wrong or is derived in a negative tone. This myth becomes your truth over time. It may be grounded in a physical reality based on the world of atoms or not. All personal truth is "real" regardless of whether it is grounded in physicality or vaporous fantasy.

The use of the words myth and delusion also remind us that one's personal narrative can be changed. No personal myth is a physical truth or set of irrefutable facts in and of itself. No delusion can be permanent. Facts are supported in various ways, and a mind can't support anything with anything other than vaporous theories, concepts, or ideas. Make no mistake, a myth can include information that is considered to be a manifest truth supported by a firm set of facts. However, this too is fundamentally the mind's conjecture. For example, a red 1967 Corvette automobile is real to both of us and a proven physical fact, but if mentally I was too frail to understand what a car was the concept of this Corvette would probably not be held within my own mind. It is your mind that validates which myths you believe and which ones you don't.

Your mind-myth develops over time, and its particular focus or degree of tilt is different than any other person who has ever lived on this planet. No one has had or ever will have your particular experiences and interpret them the same as you. Understanding the texture, tenor, or what I call the "leaning" of thoughts from either your left or right brain hemisphere is what

I am urging you to do when I speak of tasks like ultra-thinking in creation of Ultrathoughts.

Many of our decisions involving finances are made from a mind that prefers not to think about the decision. When this happens, your own "choice" will still be made, it's just that this choice is made by a mind left on autopilot. For a left-brainer like myself, autopilot decisions tend to be overly rational. For more right-brain oriented people, their automatic leaning is toward conclusions which confirm a theme of egalitarian fairness. Each prefers to ignore facts which support alternative points of view because those cause consternation within the mind. This is not an ideal situation; therefore, one should attempt to resist impulsiveness and consider all alternatives from a fair-minded perspective. A mind on autopilot is a mind which doesn't appreciate that it's engrossed in the fog of dogma.

We are each constantly justifying an existing narrative. Occasionally, we even write a new chapter. And, on still more rare occasions, we rewrite a section of the story. We tend to append pages within the existing text in a way that reconciles with our unique version of history. Naturally, the story flows smoothly when all the pages seem to belong contextually. For this reason, a person who tends to think a certain way prefers to interpret and write in that same tone.

To create a mind which is deeply contemplative is to create a mind which has confidence and opinions. Such confidence tends to work against the very idea of being fair-minded in contemplation. That's why ultra-thinking requires intent. The thinker must balance fairness and confidence. The effort necessary to be successful in pushing the mind to lean in a way other than its preferred orientation will vary. If a person has trained the mind to be accepting of alternative opinions, this mind is open and fair. I would then be inclined to call such a thinker an ultra-thinker.

The ultra-thinker is obviously different than a person who simply has a personal narrative which is constantly open to change. Such a person is simply malleable. While these are wonderful and interesting people, it is my suggestion that these folks aren't typically ultra-thinkers. Ultra-thinkers are malleable, that is true; however, they also tend to be rather opinionated. People who are constantly rewriting their own "truth" probably haven't given any truth much serious contemplation. Ultrathoughts are created by intentionally overcoming the mind's tendency to be bound by its historical point of view in hopes of enhancing the quality of truth, but this doesn't mean such ideas remain in constant flux. Opinions are fine if not encouraged provided they're kept in context. They are, however, simply delusions created by the ultra-thinker.

You might find my premise offensive simply because my own words fundamentally question your way of thinking. I've rather casually called you, and myself, by the way, a creature who lives a delusion. As you begin to notice how the mind determines relevance, you're making progress toward the creation of an Ultrathought. In fact, taking offense at my premise shall give you confidence that your personal ideology or dogma is malleable enough to at least seriously entertain my words. An absolute ideologue would rather shred this book than read it and shout me down than let me speak.

Simple awareness of ideology is not enough to overcome its influence. Yes, such mindfulness is interesting and possibly even productive to an extent, but it's not enough if you truly wish to create Ultrathoughts. The mind culls data casually and urges you to absorb only the information to which you've been primed to receive in affirmation. We *become* as we think, and those thoughts don't tend to be fair and open-minded. We seek and consume data which reinforces that which is not offensive to an existing narrative. The brain is not the internet search engine of the year 2005, a free and unfiltered exploration of alternatives. On the contrary, mind and its partner brain work as a type of Google engine of 2020; information is filtered, refined, and effectively programmed to provide what it "thinks" is best removing any and all offensive data for the simple fact that the mind *knows* best.

It's commonly accepted by neuroscientists that your attitudes and beliefs tend to coalesce as you mature. We come to present ourselves in an aura of self-created truths and opinions. Such maturation is often left to happenstance, which is likely to urge you to become more of what you are. While I will not proclaim that the very act of reflexive thinking is somehow inhuman, I do represent that to think on autopilot is akin to not thinking at all. As a species on this planet in this time and space, we apparently share one unique characteristic. We have the ability to think deep contemplative thoughts in the sixth person. To fail to use this ability, relying on a mind unchallenged, may prevent you from creating the best possible version of yourself. That, in my humble opinion, is a tragedy for both you and our society. We all succeed when we each attempt to be our best version of self.

You might be aware of research that documents that you are likely to be happier today simply by forcing yourself to smile. A physical action can create the idea of happiness within the mind, lowering your blood pressure and other stress-related physical symptoms. The converse is true as well. Your blood pressure will rise if you allow yourself to engage in a discussion that has a negative tone. This same premise applies to issues surrounding your own money impressions. You will be better

Money On A Mind

able to handle issues of personal finance simply by recognizing that in order to relieve your current money stressors you will need to change how you think, not merely increase the amount of money you have at your disposal.

Your personal story is full of pages that reflect your impressions or ideas about money, retirement, value, income taxes, asset allocation, and the stock market. Written within your mind are metaphorical pages regarding whether it's better to rent or own your home. These pages have been self-scribed reflexively or with purposeful intent as your life has unfolded. Some of your impressions may be supported by empirical data but certainly not all.

As a trained financial professional, naturally I'm inclined to promote certain financial rules of thumb: buying is better than renting, invest in your retirement plan at work, create a safety net of cash reserves. You could probably name three or four more. Of course, the truth of many of these financial rules of thumb is supported by the math; however, we must acknowledge that each of them are simply money myths at their core. They are ideas promoted within our given society and its preferred economic model.

Keeping certain money myths within my mind, I'm confident that through data I can prove it makes more sense economically to keep your four-year-old car than purchase a brand-new vehicle. I'm not unique in my proving ability. It's rather basic math. Yes, there are rare exceptions; however, most financial professionals would agree. While that's all well and good, every day hundreds of people will park perfectly good vehicles in favor of purchasing a newer, cleaner automobile they can't easily afford. Why? Because their mind has written a narrative that allows for the decision. Buyers justify their purchase by overwriting a narrative previously held—possibly one they've held for three or four years. One that said, "It would be silly to buy a car today. My old one is fine." Still, that rewrite eventually occurs in the minds of most. Typically, that rewrite includes a chapter called "I Deserve It" which reads something like, "I know it doesn't make sense and I probably can't afford this car, but I'm going to treat myself for a change." It is the mind, not common sense supported by empirical data, which drives all decisions in the end.

I point out this particular question because I'm asked something to the effect of "Should I get a new car?" at least six if not ten times every year. Each time I present some variation of the same theme. "It rarely makes financial sense to replace an older car with a new car, unless your old car is virtually unrepairable." Since a new car drops in value quicker than most any other product, they are among the worst purchases any person will make. When pressed, I'll make some calculations just to stress my point. Still, over half the time, my client soon shows up with a new vehicle. These clients value my opinion, otherwise they wouldn't have called. Yet they ignore my advice. Are they wrong?

CPAs like myself are rather known for answering a question with the phrase "it depends." Folks of my profession seek facts and figures, and we like to run the numbers. Left-brain orientation is a common characteristic found in many accountants, software engineers, and rather unfortunately for patients, physicians. Left-brainers are very comfortable believing formulas and math provide the best answers in almost every situation, and in this situation the math rarely does anything but confirm the obvious. The answer to such a logical question is, don't buy that new car. But, then again ….

As an accountant who writes books of a philosophical tone, you've probably guessed I've somewhat suppressed my natural ways of thinking. My left brain does shout, "Don't buy that new car!" Still, my right hemisphere tells me to cool it. Let's attempt to ultra-think the new car question without the biases associated with formulas of value and depreciation.

I'm rather sure it's not the best financial decision to buy a new car if your goal in life is to accumulate financial wealth. But wealth is ultimately about value, another very ill-defined idea. A thousand dollars of wealth to me is not the same as a thousand to you. My own definition or view of wealth can't really be in absolute harmony with yours even if your stated goal in life is more wealth. Furthermore, we each have multiple priorities. Driving a really cool car has been my own from time to time, as has building a financial portfolio. On second thought, an Ultrathought: Life is short, do what you want. Ultra-think the question, reconcile your actions to what you deem most important. Me, I'm looking for a deal on a brand new red Corvette.

CHAPTER 4

# MONEY MYTHS ARE SIMPLY IDEAS

Ideas that tend to create stress are very often the ideas that are most entrenched within. This happens because a mind prefers to revalidate existing views rather than recontemplate those issues which bring about anxiety and consternation. Consequently, what may have begun as a rather casual view about an important topic matures to become a stalwart belief within the mind. This type of benign validation manages to filter even the slightest hint of disagreement.

A mind is always going to be self-interested. It serves to protect both body and ego. A mind is not on some noble quest for knowledge and truth unfettered. Obviously, an easy way to protect is to shield a person from circumstances that are disagreeable. A mind which chooses its historical narrative over contemplation believes it is acting in your best interests by ignoring alternative facts. True, some minds are hungry for information. However, given a choice between information that confirms and information that threatens, the mind will typically elect to validate confirming data before the alternative. The technical phrase is "confirmation bias," and we all experience this tendency to one degree or another. Though a mind can be mastered to welcome new information which might be upsetting it takes training and self-discipline. The way you view money today will probably be the way you view it tomorrow unless you make an effort to reconsider the concept in a very fundamental way.

You can't truly turn off your money thoughts even though you may not be aware of them. They are important pages within your personal narrative simply because you've grown up in a society heavily influenced by its presence. A person who has a belief in spending tends to keep spending, while a saver saves. We are that which we believe. Over time, many of us create a thick money dogma. These beliefs, deeply held and supported by action, can be as strong as spiritual or political beliefs within the mind-myth narrative.

Most of us think of money as a *real* thing, an item of substance. After all, I've got a few bucks in my wallet this very instant. Still, if you give it some serious thought you will come to recognize that fundamentally money is an *idea*. Certainly, that idea may translate into any number of physical objects—a United States dollar, gold bullion coin, or barter item—but that doesn't change reality; money is a vaporous product of our individual minds. It's an idea that serves several functions. It's a medium of exchange and a store of value; still there's far more. Money is a concept that has been adopted by civilized *Homo sapiens* creatures, who, for whatever reason, choose to keep score, garner power, and exchange value in a manner others perceive as fair. The idea of money underpins our economic system.

No idea is purely bound to an actual material thing. An idea *can* be a representation of a physical thing, a thing of molecules, but the specific idea itself is something more. Take a physical U.S. dollar, a Federal Reserve note, from your wallet. Hold it, smell it, even scratch it with your nail. This piece of clothlike paper, the actual greenback, literally and physically exists. Let's say this particular sheet of currency even has a specific serial number: ML72539772Q. Once described in abstract and adequately described enough for the thinker to ponder in depth, it becomes an idea in addition to a material thing.

Being the case, we can continue to discuss this specific piece of paper long after the U.S. Federal Reserve shreds it due to wear and tear. After it has been shredded, this bill is physically gone, yet it remains a notion within the mind.

This specific greenback is no different from any other physical organization of atoms; every molecule of the universe will eventually deteriorate into a chaotic jumble of disorganized atoms. On the other hand, any and every idea can potentially live forever in the ether of the cosmos. This distinction defines the special nature of all ideas. Their nature goes beyond the world of atoms, though at some point they may have had physical characteristics.

To say the idea lives forever doesn't necessarily mean it lives in your reality, your world. The statement doesn't deny that this particular bill existed in a physical sense, but it does certainly imply that an idea not known is an idea that doesn't exist within your own reality. We shape all ideas of relevance including our ideas concerning money. The bill doesn't define itself and certainly doesn't mandate your own impression. Mind defines all reality to your person, but it is "relevance" that makes that reality worthy. It should be appreciated that, in fact, relevance is more important than physical existence or awareness. The relevance of money is what matters to you. If you doubt my point, hand a $100 bill to a two-year-old girl. She'll look at it briefly, but within a minute or so she'll become disinterested. The currency was meaningless to her. Was it meaningless to you, or did you squirm a bit when she started to tear it?

Money works simply because we within our given society believe it works. If we were to be magically transported back five thousand years in time, our notions of money would be irrelevant in any practical sense because we wouldn't share a common set of money beliefs with our predecessors. The ancient peoples of Sumer in modern-day Iraq had some money ideas. In fact, they may have been among the first to use gold and silver as a medium of exchange. Still, we can't be exactly sure how they thought of money. I suspect that even if I handed a common citizen of Sumer a gold bar he or she probably wouldn't have felt morally obligated to provide me with a herd of oxen in return. Their concept of money was probably far less focused on money as a store of wealth. Consequently, they wouldn't possess some intrinsic need to equalize an exchange of value. What obligation would I create today if I handed even one ounce of gold to my business partner?

Humanity has matured to consider money and wealth to be among the most important aspects of our lives. The idea of money—bits of paper, chunks of metal, or numbers on a screen—has extraordinary powers. Though each is technically worthless in themselves, they are things of value. People tend to assume that money, at least at some point, was actually worth something. Most of us consider there is some sort of difference between the worth of gold-backed currency, a gold coin or doubloon, and paper (fiat) currency. What most people don't appreciate is this "difference" is simply as meaningful or meaningless as the individual who perceives it. Fiat currency and wooden nickels are no better or worse than physical gold in your safe. They're effectively equal as long as we perceive them as equal.

There are a number of popular sayings about money, and while they may sound good, most are simply self-affirming statements promoting the views of society. Societal truth sets the tone, and individuals reflexively subscribe to the reality promoted. The foundation of the belief is mutual trust. We share a trust for fiat paper money and recognize it seems to be a fine choice for use in commerce. Some have more trust in gold than fiat as a store of value, but very few deem gold a better choice as a means of exchange. We'd then say that, overall, fiat currency is a better choice in the representation of money than gold is today. That hasn't always been the case, and it may one day change again. However, I suspect we won't go back to having more faith in gold than paper any time soon. The more likely scenario is that we soon have equal faith in crypto or digital currency as we do in fiat paper currency.

With respect to gold, it is true that the metal is often considered to have a unique money characteristic. Advocates of the metal remind us that gold has a kind of two-tier system of value: the meltdown value of the metal as a commodity and a monetary value used as a reserve selling at a fixed price. However, since governments no longer accept gold in payment, gold is actually less useful than fiat money. In a strict sense, some would say that almost every form of money could be described as having a dual purpose. You could use a wooden nickel to fuel your fireplace and tulip bulbs to produce some nice flowers. The point is that we should not be fooled by money, any form of money. Money, all money, is simply a store of value and a means of exchange to which a society has subscribed the idea of trust. Any form will work as long as at least two minds agree to this truth.

Sharing common ideas about money with others is critical to one's successful navigation of life in modern society. If a royal princess from Taiwan ends up in the wilds of the Amazon among the locals, she'd quickly learn that her own perception of wealth is of little importance. Why? No one would share her understanding of the value of her bank accounts. If she didn't reeducate herself or find a way to reeducate her local society, she'd end up facing some rather daunting challenges. Therefore, while we think our opinion of money is important, of equal importance is an appreciation of how your society is influencing your own views.

In common speaking, we tend to think of money as currency or a bank balance despite knowing that from a technical standpoint money is far more. When asked if you have "any" money or "enough" to retire, very few would pause to consider the origin of their deeply entrenched impression of money. Most of us have enough understanding to make what we believe are informed judgments about our finances but not so much as to be prepared for a finance exam. We want practical knowledge. We use that information to glean answers to questions like the following.

- Can I afford a new car?

- Will I have enough to retire when I reach my early social security retirement age?

- Would it be reckless to spend $5,000 on a vacation?

A sober mind is relied upon to provide answers to these types of questions, but can a truly accurate answer be given to any of them? It is my proclamation that they have no actual perfect answer. With that said, we will try, and indeed most will answer each of these questions at some point in their lives. We research on the web and search the mind for *the* answer, yet none of the nouns in any of these questions can be defined in absolute. Not even the number $5,000 has a consistent meaning. That amount of money means one thing to me and quite another to Bill Gates. Nouns and adjectives used in language are all heard contextually by the listener.

Money On A Mind

Let's assume you make a good amount of money per year, say $60,000, and some lender will lend you enough money to purchase your dream car, a new Porsche 718 Spyder. This is a spectacular $100,000 automobile. You're single and have a solid take-home pay of about $3,200 a month. You're not wealthy by any common standard in the U.S., and you're up to your eyeballs in credit card debt. There are a number of nouns and adjectives in these words, but you get the gist of my premise.

The payment on this new Porsche will be roughly $1,300 a month for eighty-four months, and that doesn't include mandatory insurance. You love this car and are so happy to be driving it on a beautiful winding mountain road a mere thirty miles from your home in downtown Los Angeles. While on that road on a bright Sunday morning, you glance down at your smartphone for the briefest of seconds. In an instant you smack the guardrail, breaking your neck just before the car flies off the road and tumbles down a cliff before landing on a rattlesnake that was ready to strike a baby rabbit dead. All of this happens the day before your first car payment. Were you wrong to buy the car?

This is the nature of financial decisions. You may choose a logical or even an impulsive answer. Either way, the answer you select can't be considered absolutely wrong or right until the future unfolds. No complex financial model or financial rule of thumb will ever dial you into perfection for the plain fact that every peripheral event can't be determined. Does this mean we shouldn't ponder what is an ideal answer to a financial decision? Absolutely not. We simply need to relax a bit and be aware that perfection is an illusion. And while math, statistical analysis, and expert advice can provide comfort, it's not determinative.

What we should do is focus our minds on harmonizing our decisions with the person we're attempting to create. In doing so the mind can give us comfort rather than create stress as it seeks to reconcile truths held and actions taken. Any solutions derived are utterly meaningless absent the mind's interpretation of the results. Make no mistake, I may believe certain answers are clearly wrong, but my judgment is passed within the context of the science of finance and my personal delusion filled with bias. None of my views are relevant to you unless your mind is open to considering my so-called knowledge. Science is useful to an extent, but it does not reveal some sort of hidden path to financial success. It's all about your mind, not the math.

Obviously, most of us care far more about our own money than some theoretical discussion about its nature. That's why we hire bean counters and subscribe to financial newsletters more often than listen to the musings of philosophers. With due respect, this highlights the challenge. We can hardly resist the urge to think of money as a physical thing and that there is some way to win at the game of money. Unfortunately, the game people tend to think they're playing is simply a delusion to which they subscribe. Your impression of this thing, not the tangible sense of value you've convinced yourself that you own, is all that is truly important. Money, all of it, is an idea which can appear to be a kind of game that can be won, but it is actually just a pure idea.

It is through an exploration of the very nature of all ideas that you will come to appreciate what your mind is doing. You'll come to appreciate how your mind has an impression of value and weaves it within its views of other related ideas. Understand what you value and you can understand money. Understand money and you can better decide whether you should work in your current job, pay taxes to your political leaders, save, spend, and long for retirement, or not.

You are the collection of views you've organized in the mind. Financial decision-making with regards to personal finance has to do with your impressions of money, current mood, perceived social status, and lifestyle. We may share many views and probably think of reality in pretty much the same way. We both read the English language and even file a U.S. income tax return once a year. However, the depth of our individual narratives makes it literally impossible for us to perceive each and every aspect of life the same way. You have your style and me, my own. I have my risk tolerance with regard to loss of value and you have yours. Upon fair evaluation, neither of us is more correct than the other despite the fact one of us may have more *facts* on our side. Why? Because when it comes to ideas, no fact is relevant to another when that person fails to believe it so. There are no absolute truths, therefore I cannot judge the worthiness of your own.

Money becomes a contextual thing intermingled within your personal narrative. Your mind hears, interprets, and refines the concept each waking day. The whole process tends to function at a subconscious level. Views tend to be reflexive, born of a mind distracted and left on autopilot. Obviously, a distracted pilot is not an ideal pilot. Therefore, we can assume the money ideas most of us harbor are probably not particularly well-conceived.

Before attempting to ultra-think your ideas surrounding money, how to keep it, spend it, earn it, or even waste it, I suggest you start by asking yourself a very basic, yet quite profound question: "What is the very nature of any idea, including my own idea of money?" This single question should be asked by every thinking person on the planet regardless of issues of money. To ask and seriously consider this question will help you build an appreciation of the ideas, concepts, and themes which create your own version of reality.

CHAPTER 5

# PHILOSOPHICALLY SPEAKING

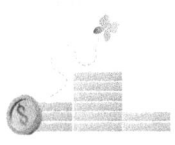

Ideas themselves are curious things. They seem to be an innate feature of what we know as our physical existence, however, they themselves are unbound by the world of atoms. Plato was among the first of whom we are aware to have explored the concept that a "thing" could still be *something* absent physicality. An idea can be simply a nonphysical presence, a "meta" thing. A full exploration of Plato is above my paygrade, but in brief, I'll attempt to summarize his Ultrathoughts on the meta (nonphysical) realm versus the physical realm.

Plato's interpretation of the nature of things is explained through his monumental theory of forms. He theorized that forms are things in and of themselves. They can exist apart from the objects they describe. For instance, the word *apple* can mean a natural fruit made of physical atoms, or a shape, a thing having no atoms at all. The shape of an apple can be imagined without visualizing the fruit. Therefore, *apple* is a quality of its own form. It can be the real, physical apple or a potential form of abstract thought. Since the abstract thought of *apple* is grounded in representation based on the physical apple, it is a quality. To say that something has an apple shape is to represent a form without the specific object. *Apple* has a metaphysical presence.

Contrast a physical object and its representation with something like the word *beautiful* as in the phrase "a beautiful sunset." Beauty is a form having an existence, yet it will never be comprised of atoms nor will it specifically represent any physical object. Though we can ponder beauty in the abstract as we can apple, we could never describe beauty as being tied to a specific object in representation. We won't always agree that a sunset is an absolute beauty, unlike our agreement on the shape of an apple. Note the difference, and then contemplate the implication of the distinction between an idea of beauty and an idea of an apple in shape.

Plato, through his Theory of Forms, explores the nature of things and attempts to bring structure to concepts that deal with what is real. "Real" can, therefore, be meta real or physically real. Ultrathoughts of this type document what we consider the earliest detailed descriptions of the nature of reality. Before one can attempt to contemplate the nature of reality, one must create a foundational definition. Plato's Theory of Forms provides us with that foundation.

While Plato provided a foundational theory of the meaning of an idea, it was left to hundreds if not thousands of others to build on this work. English philosopher John Locke (1632–1704) was certainly no contemporary of Plato, who lived about two thousand years earlier. Locke was less interested in the foundation of philosophy than whether ideas themselves exist apart from human comprehension. As a Protestant Christian who rejected the idea that the clergy speaks for God, he sought to understand whether human beings are absolutely free creatures with respect to their personal actions and obligations to their God.

Locke created his own Ultrathought, his *theory of mind*. He maintained that human beings have absolutely no innate bias from their God other than morality. God made individuals moral beings, unlike common animals. Morality is an idea from God; therefore, absent evil influences, a rationally thinking human will be fair in their own actions.

Unlike morality, knowledge itself is obtained, not granted from on high. Knowledge is evaluated and determined worthy or not within the context of personal experience by the individual. God does not dictate action but has granted us liberty and free will. Naturally, personal liberty allows people to make honest errors in judgment and to even rationalize a patently immoral act. Morality exists in absolute, but though we've been granted this gift of awareness, we'll always remain flawed interpreters of information. Human creatures make mistakes in offense of God-given morality. In the view of Locke, these mistakes aren't ideal, but they are certainly expected by an all-knowing God.

Locke was a scientist to his core. He believed something must be capable of being tested, otherwise, it was in fact nothing to begin with. In *An Essay Concerning Human Understanding*, he refined the concept of self. He determined that humans are generally self-interested creatures. They will not inherently defer to the interest of the collective group because they understand they have been granted privilege by their God, not their earthly leaders.

Fairness, morality, and reason are concepts further explored by another philosopher and economist, Adam Smith (1723–1790). Though Locke explored the idea of liberty and freedom, it was left to Smith to effectively describe the workings of what he believed was the reality of an economy that works for free individuals. Prior to the era of Locke and Smith, what economic theory there was largely centered on ideas promoted by aristocratic rulers. Decisions were made for people because they hadn't been considered at liberty to choose much of anything for themselves. The needs of the masses of common folk were rarely considered in a feudalistic economic model where land barons and nobles acted as agents of kings, queens, church, and state. The ideas of Locke and Smith urged people to reconsider the historical truth of society.

Respecting that Locke had proven human beings were at liberty to make free choices, Smith explored how such freedoms impact society and economics. He brought forth Ultra-thoughts around these subjects in what came to be called a *free market economic theory*.

Without a doubt, free markets have existed since the dawn of civilization; still, they weren't common on a scale like we're accustomed to today. Controlled markets offer more opportunities for manipulation to the advantage of the powerful. Local leaders, landlords, nobles, and well-heeled merchants maintained these orderly markets and had a vested interest in the status quo. Free markets often encourage chaos, and a principal point of an authoritarian government is to squelch chaos. I surmise this is one of many reasons why free markets tended to be discouraged.

Slowly the public, and reluctantly their political leaders, came to appreciate the ideas of personal liberty, and with that the idea that personal choice just may be an inalienable right. People might not be bound by class at birth, but just may be born free. What does that idea of freedom mean within the context of a merchant market, and what impact does that have on the economy of a nation?

Adam Smith was a professor and philosopher who theorized how money, value, and choice work within the dynamics of such a free society. In his most important work, *The Wealth of Nations*, he wrote what would become a kind of economics textbook for government leaders and business folks alike. He explained when, how, and why he assumes consumers are free, rational, and self-interested creatures. When they engage in an economic transaction, absent other force, they will seek to maximize value. In doing so they foster competition, which in turn increases the efficiency of production leading to surplus value. This added value, added as a result of freedom, enhances a nation that encourages freedom. The value held within a nation is more than its tangible wealth. It includes the value of an idea or concept known as a "free market." Value itself is circular and self-sustaining. Value created, creates more by the very act. Governments should restrain their impulses to control markets and encourage more freedom.

Smith further concluded that the ultimate worth of any given nation is best defined not by its gold, timber, livestock, or other resources but from the potential value to be created by its citizens. Free citizens operating within a free market create the most possible value. Therefore, any country's value is enhanced through the promotion of actions in respect of such freedom. National interests are optimized when they are aligned with citizens' interests.

The way Smith viewed things, it was obvious that regulation and government-imposed structure suppresses value creation. The government should have confidence in the consumer and encourage consumption. When this is done, the consumer can't help but add wealth to the society. Sellers also benefit from having self-interested consumers who can shop between vendors. This creates competition, which spurs improvement and product differentiation, creating more wealth in the process.

Free markets helped everyone in Smith's view. The consumer is satisfied in exercising choice, sellers are rewarded for offering superior value or products, and government is pleased by economic growth and tax dollars collected. Both a happy customer and profitable seller give credit to government leaders. A free and fair market is the ultimate win.

Smith's ideas seem to serve as a baseline theory from which our economy operates in the United States. With very few exceptions, most citizens of the Western hemisphere, Australia, and Western Europe subscribe to the economic model described so well by Adam Smith. Furthermore, within the past fifty years or so, a somewhat restricted outline of this theory has spread across the globe. Described but not invented by Smith, these free market concepts form much of our personal money narrative.

We reflexively assume we have the freedom to shop and are to be rewarded for being self-interested in seeking to maximize value. Shopping creates more value. Creation is good, and shopping is good for the self and government. Few among us go through our day without considering what is an equitable exchange of value. This theory is in operation even in countries like Vietnam and Nepal. Consumers select a Sherpa to take them up Mount Everest by negotiating a fee based on the idea of a free market pricing model which maximizes value to the benefit of all. This outline of value exchange and wealth storage is core to our own broad money myth.

When people across cultures think of money the same way, they can work together to forge a global economy despite the fact they have drastically different outlooks on a number of other issues. Mortal enemies still purchase food and supplies from each other via a free market system. Efficiency is the key advantage to the theory so well described by Adam Smith. It is for this reason even communist governments allow for free market exchange even though their own political system is far from one which promotes personal liberty.

It is certainly no revelation to point out that a free market economy is not "good" for all members of society. How can the mentally ill be expected to conduct a free market exchange?

How can a person whose only value worth exchanging is manual labor possibly live comfortably when they throw out their back and can't work? Yes, critics say, maybe a free market is efficient, but it is not a "fair" market. Don't we, as humans, seek fairness above value transfer and wealth creation?

Karl Marx, born in 1818 in Trier, Germany, seemed to strive for institutionalized fairness. The fairness he contemplated was considered broadly. It included ideas of society, government, and economics. Like many critics of free market capitalism, in principle, he understood the theory that competition urges the construction of better goods and fosters an environment that can enhance the human experience. He understood the model created new value and facilitated the transfer of stored human value to the benefit of common folk. Like Smith, Marx despised aristocratic control and feudalism, but unlike his predecessor, he wasn't optimistic that capitalists themselves were any better. They, like nobility, would exploit their advantage over any given worker.

Though he would never be considered a philosopher whose depth of thought rivaled the likes of Smith, Voltaire, or Hegel, Marx was brilliant and used his intellect well, coming to study philosophy at a young age. He was an enthusiastic student and writer who was attracted to egalitarian concepts. He joined the Poets' Club while attending the University of Bonn. The group was monitored by the police at the time. Despite the watchful eye of authority, he continued to write both fiction and nonfiction pieces. He wrote poetry, though none of his poems were published during his lifetime. As time passed, he became attracted to more serious matters. His doctoral thesis, written in his early twenties, dealt with the idea that theology is inherently inferior to philosophy. Marx was an atheist.

After his education, he became a co-editor of what was considered a very radical newspaper. When this authorized paper eventually collapsed, he found himself writing for an underground publication which promoted the idea that people should build a utopian society populated by laborers and artisans. Eventually, he became stateless as a result of his vocal criticism of prominent aristocrats. It was during this period that he sought a deeper understanding of the workings of capitalism and contrasted these ideas with those of people like Friedrich Hegel.

Marx was more of a promoter than a pure thinker like Plato, Locke, or Smith. Smith, the professor, was content to theorize. He preferred to operate within an academic setting and actually published very little. Marx was not a behind-the-scenes sort of fellow. He thought, wrote, and overtly advocated for social justice as he saw it. He certainly didn't invent the ideas of socialism or collectivism. He didn't even invent the idea we associate with him: Marxism. In fact, the term wasn't even used in his lifetime. The word Marxism is associated with a highly controlled socioeconomic model which presupposes that individual liberty must be sacrificed for the benefit of the collective group. This concept was co-opted and branded as Marxism by certain dictators and elitists in an attempt to soften their message: Bow to the wisdom of your leaders for the good of us all.

To call Marx a promotor doesn't deny that he had significant depth of thought. From his own ultra-thinking and self-study, it seemed rather obvious that, in terms of value, the worker typically was asked to sacrifice theirs to the benefit of both landlord and factory owner. Each was far more powerful than any single working individual, and when push came to shove, each common worker would give up far more than they ever received in return.

The way Marx viewed things, the only effective way to protect the worker was for workers to unite as a block. Consequently, an individual was better off in the long run by sacrificing personal liberty to join with peers rather than to attempt to fight what would always be a losing battle alone. A person's maximized value potential is never achieved as an individual, period. Workers must stand firm in unity. Furthermore, the group should not allow any individuals to defect or they would risk their own maximized value. Coercion against a defector is justified and is in the best interests of both the individual and the collective.

Marx knew that the success of a large and complex country ultimately depended on the value of its resources. Like Smith, he viewed citizens and the value they stored as a resource of the country. Countries and their leaders had no real choice other than to convert this value into production, while capitalists were simply self-interested. The commoner was constantly being exploited by capitalists who truly had no rights to this resource at all. In his view, it was foolish to assume that a free market would eventually work all of this out equitably; therefore, it was left to the government to set up systems to remedy the situation.

Marx didn't despise the theory of capitalism as many assume. He wrote about how it brought about progress and economic growth. However, he also believed that pure capitalism and free market economies can't help but encourage imbalance. Capitalism (free markets run by capitalists) will ultimately lead to periods of booms and busts. While booms are great for all, only the worker experiences the true effect of a bust. Left unchecked, societies based on capitalism will devolve toward what we call crony capitalism.

In the view of Marx, only a "new communist society" could assure fairness, protect the masses, and maximize value. A government must dictate fairness from the top down rather than letting its citizens be victims of a heartless capitalist system underpinned by an illusion of a fair and free market. Government, done well, can create a utopia for all citizens of the world. Though the transition might be painful, a universal utopia and its creation are necessary to ensure that the downtrodden aren't victimized. Once accomplished, all involved are ahead. The government maximizes the value of its resources, and a collective group of human creatures lives a utopian existence.

Note the fundamental difference in focus between the views of Marx (collectivism) and those of Smith (individualism). Smith spoke of maximizing the wealth of nations and benefit to the country, but he was restrained by his fundamental belief that an individual is special in the eyes of his God. Therefore, he was reluctant if not prohibited from having individuals sacrifice themselves for the broader economic interest of the group or country. Obviously, a team of horses working together produces more value than the individuals in isolation, but Smith didn't think of people as just another resource like timber or livestock. Humans are more than just resources—we're privileged beings. Therefore, the very idea of collective value with respect to human beings was not considered. Marx, on the other hand, had no such belief. An individual was simply another beast of burden in his view.

There we have it. Two broad economic models: free market capitalism presupposing the special nature of any individual person, and controlled market socialism which assumes it is proper to sacrifice individual benefit for the greater good. I would say the worst devolution of capitalism is crony capitalism where favoritism dominates, and the worst devolution of a controlled market is a bureaucratic aristocracy that nurtures its own existence as it starves citizens. Some minds have decided that, given we are free beings, we should be able to freely engage in economic transactions without much oversight. Others believe it is best for our society to compromise a bit more of our individual liberty for the greater good of society.

Which system is best? I have my favorite, but I've little doubt my views are still very biased, so I'm hesitant to call mine an Ultrathought. My own narrative is laced with the theories of Smith more than Marx. Still, I freely admit either economic model is valid and has its pros and cons.

CHAPTER 6

# SOCIETY AND MONEY IDEAS

Economic systems are refined based on the particular dynamics of their society. This evolution is not always linear. Economic systems, like almost everything else with regards to society, seem to exist on a metaphorical pendulum. When the system moves too far toward crony capitalism, market participants rebel and demand more regulation. When buyers and sellers become overburdened by controls, they demand deregulation, and when action doesn't occur they simply leave the marketplace altogether, often moving to black markets. Economic systems may be manipulated by buyers, sellers, cronies, or regulators, but they aren't dictated from an all-knowing eye in the sky. They are simply systems created and managed by people who themselves are confined within their given society.

The economic systems of Western Europe, Australia, and North America are grounded in what most would characterize as a free market-based economy. Their citizens take for granted the ideas of Smith and are barely aware of the competing ideas espoused by Marx. Government under capitalism does regulate key aspects of economic transactions, but for the most part, it tends to assume that given enough time competition will encourage fairness. Key to the idea and well explained by Smith is that individuals are fundamentally moral. Though people act in their own best interests, they aren't so concerned with their own self-interest that they will harm another for the sake of a few dollars. The capitalist system seems to work reasonably well, though there is no denying that if morality breaks down within a society this economic model will not work for long.

As most know, the economic system in a country like China is quite different. Their economy is tightly choreographed on a macro (large-scale) level. Yes, in some markets there is ample competition, and for all practical purposes these are free-but-monitored markets. Shops advertise sale prices and offer special value all with the blessings of the government, not too dissimilar from any market in Western society. In China, people are assumed to be self-interested as they are in the United States. However, the very idea of "self-interest" is not the same in China as we think of it in the U.S.

We tend to believe self-interest is fine and good. In fact, it is a sign of a person's high moral character to engage in an equitable transaction. We rarely expect anything for free and seek to compensate "fairly" for goods and services. To be fair in commerce is to be personally moral. To take advantage in a transaction is to act immorally. With regard to consumer markets, this belief is not shared across the globe. If a merchant can take advantage of a customer in a bazaar in a Middle Eastern country they will. They are not considered an immoral cheater but a wise and skillful merchant.

This rather fluid view of morality isn't unique to the areas outside of Western society. What is different between societies is when and where a society pins personal morality to a market and when it doesn't. For example, the most successful hedge fund manager in Manhattan is probably one of the better liars in their market, just like the wealthiest merchant in a Middle Eastern bazaar. In the strictest of sense, neither within a certain context is any more a liar than you or I. Am I a liar when I spruce up my home for a top-dollar sale? After all, I did use the brightest of light bulbs to disguise that rather dark corner of the living room. How about that time I took advantage of a merchant desperate for cash to stave off bankruptcy? Am I just as immoral as the corporate raider on Wall Street? Issues of morality and money are complicated, which is why it's extremely difficult to balance personal morality and economic transactions.

In theory, ideas of money and morality should operate in two entirely different spheres. However, this is definitely not the case. As with all ideas, it is the mind-myth narrative of the thinker which ultimately determines where the dividing line is drawn between the two. I can consider myself moral while beating a merchant at his game yet call a person a crook when they fail to pay my invoice for services rendered.

When we consider a Marxist society like that of the Chinese, it is important to appreciate just how different their culture is than our own. Their entire sense of morality is different. Don't misunderstand my point. The Chinese citizen is as moral as any other human on this planet, but their interpretation of this morality is weighted toward what's in the interest of the group. Like their language to the ears of a typical American, we can't automatically understand this foreign tone of morality. How could a Chinese employee ever think it was righteous to literally steal the copyright of a musician or a patent held by a corporation?

The confusion is mutual. They don't understand how we think. Why would we ever sacrifice the dignity and benefit of our country in favor of putting a few more dollars in our wallet? How could we keep a patent for a life-changing technology a secret simply because we had the money to hire an attorney to fill out some paperwork? What if that patent was for a drug that saved the lives of billions? Is this patent worth a billion lives within a society or a trillion dollars in the bank account of a drug maker?

These fundamental differences in interpretation of truth and morality are why when a Chinese business person "steals" technological secrets from another citizen or an American company the Chinese don't necessarily believe they've done anything immoral. In fact, laws in China might even encourage such action simply because the theft would benefit the broader Chinese society. Their laws don't recognize the proprietary prerogative of an inventor against the interest of an entire society. A Chinese citizen shall always strive to be moral, but they have a duty to the collective and the state first and foremost. An American citizen has no such obligation. We may be inclined to act in the best interest of the group, but most of us won't consider this an obligation and certainly wouldn't typically sacrifice our personal sense of honor for the good of the state.

The fairness of any transaction is a judgment left to law, state, and societal opinion. A law commands citizens to act within codified norms. The Chinese system of government, like many outside of the United States, the European Union, and Australia, doesn't assume an inalienable right to freedom within its legal code. They don't agree with the ideas of people like John Locke and don't believe freedom has anything to do with a gift from the Godhead. Freedom, and the liberty to exercise it, is a right granted by the government. With regard to market transactions, people aren't free unless they are approved to be so. Consumers granted such rights may buy any approved product, but citizens don't have a God-given right to anything, not even water. All are granted by the government and economic privileges earned.

Every country is different, and it should be acknowledged that the United States does not have the freest of "free markets." Countries, all of them, regulate some aspects of their economy and markets. If they didn't, they'd have no way to collect tax revenue, assure the safety of citizens, and protect the environment from profiteers. Still, there is grave disagreement between intelligent and thoughtful people regarding where to start and stop regulating.

When an economy becomes more and more regulated, a free market model of capitalism takes on what many call a socialist's tone. The freestyle dance of a business transaction described by Smith morphs into a highly choreographed routine supervised by societal leaders. As they say, the devil is in the details. One person's necessary and useful regulation is often deemed by another as a self-serving if not sinister manipulation of people and markets. There are very few truly free markets. I can come close, but frankly, I can't tell you I know of any that are absolutely free.

Governments exist to serve people, society, and, yes, themselves. Government being concerned about government isn't bad. Frankly, we need governments to do more than exist. Governments should prosper like the people they serve. Governments must impose structure and rule to meet its broader objective, to manage a society of people who have competing interests. As rules and regulations become more intrusive, we note they tend to move toward the model of socialism, and when regulations are removed, they move more toward capitalism.

When people choose to think of a specific country, they tend to assume its economic environment can be characterized as being either that of free market capitalism or controlled market socialism. That is a misunderstanding. Countries are not either-or but a blend. Different markets within a country are regulated differently. For instance, the United States has a very free market with regards to, say, avocados but a very regulated market regarding milk production. We could then say we have avocado-capitalism and milk-socialism. Why is this the case?

Though I'm sure someone can provide dozens of reasons that milk is more regulated than avocados, for purposes of this discussion the minutiae doesn't matter. The ultimate reason why our government regulates the milk market more is that the members of the society of the United States want milk regulated to a higher degree than avocados. Members of a society, their elected leaders, or their ruling elite determine the preferred economic model for a given country and ultimately for any particular market. There is no correct or incorrect answer with regard to a type of market. There is no manifest truth regarding what is a perfect economic model or a model deemed righteous by the cosmos. These ideas simply exist within the minds of human beings.

Every society presents a tone—a mind of society. Citizens tend to share beliefs common among their members. These beliefs, ideas, or truths lead to the reality of the society. Societal beliefs create a kind of force or peer pressure. Societies evolve to trust their economy and its financial concepts. As our global society becomes more cohesive, its economic beliefs have moved toward homogenization. Most citizens of the United States wouldn't have hesitated to conduct an economic transaction with a person who lives in Germany or Australia in the 1970s. They would not have been so likely to have trust in a transaction based in China. Today that is not the case. Most consumers, internationally, trust that their global transactions will be handled in a fair and equitable manner. Naturally, that trust is not absolute. If we had a hint that our German partner was dishonest, we'd quickly decide to go elsewhere with our economic transaction.

As each day goes by, it's safe to assume that, in a pejorative sense, our trust in the global economy grows as long as no negative events are observed. Certainly, some of us are more skeptical than others, but most citizens don't think much about the economy. We take for granted it will work tomorrow because it worked today. Those in India, Ecuador, and France basically do the same. They generally trust the system, otherwise, they would not engage with customers and vendors from abroad.

Obviously, levels of trust vary. Citizens of Venezuela have been economically "burned" far more often than citizens from the United States. As a result, their level of trust in any economic system is far less than that of the citizens of the U.S. Still, they must have some degree of trust; otherwise, they'd be entirely left out of the global economy.

Faith to one degree or another is the single common key to every system. Any system is simply an idea based on a set of other concepts. A shared set of beliefs must be somewhat agreed upon by participants if any game is to be played at all. I can't be playing checkers when you're playing poker. Still, I must admit that given the fluidity of our rules variation within the game is allowed.

Each society has its assumptions about money and the workings of an economy. For instance, in the U.S. we tend to think it's a good thing to own a home rather than rent. In general, our society may think of this as a manifest truth, but certainly it is not. That said, the belief is supported by certain economic realities that have been rather common recently. Long-term inflation trends, population growth, and the benefit of financial leverage add credence to the idea of ownership being the best choice. Still, these trends won't continue forever, so we can never proclaim with absolute certainty that it's best to buy rather than rent.

We have created dozens of these so-called financial "truths" within the mind. In the U.S., most of us aspire to retire at some point. We seem to have this idealized view that we should each simply live out our final years without the obligations of formal employment. Another view we tend to share is that it is a noble thing for parents to sacrifice their wealth for the benefit of their children's college education. Are any of these assumptions a manifest truth or even a noble thing to do? Of course not. They are myths which may be supported by mathematics within a given context, but they're never actual truths of the cosmos.

Key to so many of our broader beliefs and faiths is the global acceptance of the U.S. dollar as a reserve currency. Dollar faith is a cornerstone to our society and has a great deal to do with how smoothly the global economic system has worked for the past seventy-five years. Without equivocation, most who know economics would assume that if the U.S. dollar lost its reputation the dollar would collapse in value within a few months. This one single change in societal opinion would bring about major changes to the entire global economic system. Will faith be lost in the dollar in the next two, five, or ten years? I don't think that is likely at all, but it could happen tomorrow. Ideas are concepts having no absolute grounding. Will a collapse of the U.S. dollar happen within a few hundred years? Of course it will. The mind of society does change.

CHAPTER 7

# DEBT AND THE IMPRUDENT IDEA OF LENDING TO GOD

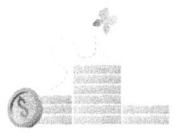

Recently, a theme has been enthusiastically promoted. Books and articles are consistently referring to something like a "great reset" to come with respect to the U.S. dollar. Authors speculate that any day now U.S. money—and with it the economic reputation of the United States—will go from first to worst. They often point to the amount of U.S. government debt issued as being the main impetus for the coming collapse. When they're reminded that the U.S. is simply doing what every other global economic powerhouse is doing, they embellish their overall thesis. They frequently infer that the aggressive promotion of our Western way of life will come back to haunt us. In a kind of cosmic sense, our societal narrative is too arrogant. The United States will be taken down a notch or two, and its citizens will feel the pain—economically speaking.

Though I don't believe the universe keeps score and punishes, per se, it is possible these authors will be proven correct. I've read way too many of these nihilistic books myself and really have to stay on guard, not letting too many zombie apocalypse themes pin within my own narrative. With bias admitted, maybe our paychecks *will* all be rendered meaningless one Friday afternoon in August 202X. Only time will tell. Still, in my view, reconsidered through ultra-thinking, there will be no one specific U.S. dollar collapse absent an extraneous event like a solar flare or meteor strike. I think we're more likely to have a kind of slow reset. Make no mistake, everyone loses in this either way, slow or sudden.

Those who see the U.S. dollar as the problem point to the rapid increase in the amount of debt issued as a principle cause. They spout off the trillions and point to graphs as they tell us the debt is unsustainable. True, the rate of increase in the debt graphs clearly shows the trajectory isn't sustainable. The debt of tomorrow won't be repaid. In fact, the debt of today or even yesterday won't be repaid either. We are, by all rights, bankrupt as a country. However, what the forecasters of doom often fail to bring up is that virtually every other sovereign nation is worse off, fiscally speaking, than the United States.

So, as long as we *are* the world's printing press, the fact the country is in debt beyond belief might just be utterly irrelevant. The strength of a currency, and indeed confidence in a currency, is a relative judgment. We don't have to be great or even good; frankly, we can have an absolutely awful currency provided there is a common belief that the U.S. is better than the alternatives. Until the globe finds a better way to "reserve" value, the U.S. dollar will remain king. The economic interests of the globe are served by continuing to honor this one king, at least for now.

Our dominant position in the world's economy will eventually come to an end. I suspect this end will have nothing do with the universe seeking to punish us evil citizens. It will probably occur when major economies decide to use some sort of "basket" or index of currencies rather than our one currency as the standard measure. Regardless, when it does occur, the U.S. consumer will fair poorly simply because we've been the biggest beneficiaries. Those who have the most to lose will lose more. For years we've reaped the benefits of U.S. economic dominance. We've seen our lifestyles improve on the heels of price declines in any number of product sectors: furniture, clothing, electronics, household items … the list is massive. This will change. It's only a matter of time.

The citizens of the United States are the world's number one customer by far. We are responsible for a third or more of the planet's economic activity. Other consumers are important and are growing in importance, but since U.S. consumers are largely unrestrained, when we create wealth we're at liberty to transfer it to others. We are both the beneficiaries and facilitators of a free market economy. As facilitators, we have a kind of special status among customers worldwide. We are the first and best customer, but more importantly, we are the creating customer. What country can afford to stifle the U.S. consumer, whose freedom to buy literally keeps markets vibrant and competitive? We make the system work, for now.

Nations and companies operate sub-economies under the broader global system. They make decisions that balance their specific needs against the health of the system in general. When the system is healthy, they can act with impunity. When the system is frail, they must compromise their goals in favor of keeping the whole thing afloat. Whether it's the European Union being reluctant to clamp down on the debts of Spain or German bankers failing to foreclose on Greek national debt, it appears giant lenders don't want to foreclose on huge borrowers. They don't want to actually acknowledge when and if a debt goes bad because in doing so they must report the default and record the loss on their books. To record a loss is to admit failure. They seem to prefer to attempt to manage a problem rather than fix it. It's safe to assume they do so because they believe it's best in the long run.

In the Great Recession of 2008, we started hearing the phrase "too big to fail." While there are very few who actually are *that* big, given what they call contagion risk, one failure can start a domino of multiple failures. Multiple failures jeopardize the system. I suspect there are an incredible number of "too big" countries, companies, and maybe even a couple dozen individuals who'd meet this definition. I suspect Jeff Bezos and his company Amazon are too big to fail.

This concept, that a borrower can be too big to let fail, informs me that a hoard of relatively small nonpaying borrowers would fall into that same category. This is what happened during the housing crisis a few years ago. Lenders and indeed their insurer, the U.S. government, couldn't let the masses fail in unison, so they moved judiciously with foreclosure proceedings. When things get so bad that everyone is in financial trouble, no collection can be enforced. As the saying goes, "When you owe the bank a little money, it owns you. When WE owe the bank or government a lot of money, WE own it."

Having this as my outline, it seems the global economic system won't let the U.S. consumer fail quickly. Therefore, there will not be an actual great reset occurring within a period of a few days in some future year. Lenders can't force an immediate and drastic reset nor overtly replace the U.S. dollar without destroying themselves in the process. We are the system. That said, when the dollar becomes merely a component of the larger basket of currencies, we as a nation will default on a substantial portion of our debt. This will occur, but it will happen over a period of years, and those years are on the horizon.

Of course, who am I? I'm just an accountant in Arizona. So if you want to agree with those who are expecting a great reset, fine. It really makes little difference. The specifics of the fall are less important than the fall itself anyway.

Economists and experts inform us that debt will be our downfall as a nation. Too bad. I mean, we really love our debt.

## Money On A Mind

We love the idea of debt about as much or maybe more than the idea of money itself. We subscribe to the idea that each is good, but at least so far, we also subscribe to the idea that debt *should* be repaid in good faith. Unless, of course, the bastard didn't deserve the repayment.

Recall the story of Honest Abe, our most noble U.S. president. Didn't he walk six miles to return a penny or something like that? Certainly, he would have paid his debts in each and every circumstance, but would he have walked seven miles to return that particular penny? How about a hundred miles? Would that unfortunate merchant who gave too much change to Abe simply have been short a penny if Abraham Lincoln had not felt like walking for a couple of weeks? This is the nature of morality issues. Morality is perceived by people within a specific context of mind. Issues of money don't seem to fit in quite the same way. He's honest when he walks a mile, but in my view good ole Abe would be quite the fool to walk a hundred.

Just the other day a former client cheated me out of some money. Like the U.S. government who knows the debt won't be repaid, this client literally misled me in a way that was intentional. They did so to their monetary advantage and at my own expense of $146.17. Shall I shrug this crime off given my own declaration of the very nature of morality? Yes, I will. Why? Because life is a quest for peace of mind. In context, this injustice simply isn't worth the toll on my body. I'm choosing not to get myself worked up about this particular event. Had they victimized me for two, three, or four times more … that is another matter. But this week I'll leave the person of less than stellar character at peace.

This is what will happen when the U.S. government defaults. The government will justify their behavior, as I'm sure that client did in my own case, and their vendor (participants in the global economy) will shrug it off. It's simply business. Best global business practices would be to let a government—whether it's Spain, Greece, or the U.S.—default. So when the global system fails, life will go on. No zombie apocalypse needed. The system will evolve, and when it does there will be something else yet to be determined. That is not to say you and I won't feel economic hardship. We will and need to ponder the details, but the world will go on, and eventually, as the new paradigm normalizes, things will be fine enough.

Make no mistake, I am no model of human virtue. I've kept a few coins, unlike my favorite president. Still, I do believe in a kind of cosmic morality. So I'm not inclined to keep a gain not considered fairly earned within my own mind. I've also never walked away from a debt, not yet anyway. Call it dharma, call it a belief in the protestant work ethic, the description is unimportant. Though the universe doesn't exact revenge, it does seem to operate in a manner that favors righteous acts. I think it's best to keep my life morally harmonized with my own concept of universal good. I'll never prove my point; still, I ultra-think we humans possess some type of innate moral compass. Therefore, I think most of us are in 90% agreement about what's morally correct. I'm quite confident that no one learned that it's wrong to destroy with abandon. We were born having an innate sense of good. As physical creatures we attempt to balance those instincts against the pressures of daily existence.

Now, add that innate understanding to the fact that we each are members of a society that helps further define morality, and we end up being in agreement more like 99.9% of the time. Peer pressure serves to keep us in line. People who live in the same society share a common morality. Some of that shared sense of morality has to do with our mutual appreciation of standards related to economic transactions and a societal money narrative. We'll act morally when we shop at the self-serve kiosk at the grocer, but we'll listen keenly in hopes of hearing that insider stock tip. You and I share a general assumption about what is a "fair" and what is a "dishonest" act, still our agreement is not absolute. We defer final judgment to laws and leaders when need be; regardless, one's true moral character can't be judged by anyone other than the individual.

A prime example in representation of my beliefs occurred during the U.S. housing crisis of 2007–2012. Some folks who seemingly have high moral standards simply chose to walk away from debt that they probably could have paid because they considered themselves victimized by bankers. It might have been a struggle, but they could have made their house payments. Others of equally high character chose to stick it out, making incredible sacrifices to pay the debt on their homes. This second group may have been as much a victim as the first. After all, it is well-documented that there were unscrupulous lender tactics used which effectively tricked homeowners into borrowing way more than they could repay comfortably. My question to you: Are the payers of debt more moral than those who walked away?

Let me pause to give you some insight into my own mind-myth of ideas. The fundamental premise of a debt transaction is an exchange of value for the purpose of profit. Lending is a business transaction. The borrower initiates a request for a transaction. The lender assumes the risk involved in the loan with an expectation of compensation in the form of interest charged. Since compensation is involved in this business arrangement, it would not be a "moral failure" if the debt is not repaid. This idea is a business-related notion whose morality is subrogated to legal authority. For this reason, default (non-repayment of debt) or bankruptcy (limited protection from forced collection) is not a reflection of personal character in my reality. Smart and moral folks often default on loan obligations and even declare bankruptcy, as do fools and heathens. Such is the right of each under the law. When a loan is agreed upon with interest or other consideration, a promise based purely on faith that it will be repaid becomes a legal contract based on law. It is an economic transaction. I'll expand upon my own mind-myth narrative appreciating that you may vehemently disagree.

Let's assume you are a lender and God walks into your office. He asks for a loan on an investment property. Jane, at more or less the same time asks for a similar loan. You only have enough funds to grant one loan. I suggest it would be wise to turn down God. Why? He would be less likely to do what is prudent business-wise because his moral character trumps all other decisions. He certainly wouldn't kick a tenant out for nonpayment of rent. Consequently, God would be more likely to go into default. To make matters worse, he certainly won't help in the repossession of a piece of real estate currently occupied by a family who's unable to pay their bills.

The fact that interest is paid on a loan changes the character of this promise from an issue of cosmic morality to a business issue. Let's go deeper. We'll assume I lent money to both God and Jane for their investment properties. Both loans went in default. Jane, the good business person she is, kicked out the nonpaying tenant in favor of signing over the secured property held as collateral on the loan I made to her. God simply couldn't do this. He let the family stay in the property, and as a result, I could not get fair restitution on my loan. I, in turn, lost my own business, went bankrupt, my wife walked out on me as a result of our personal financial drama, and, unable to manage my own despair, I become drug-addicted living in your garage. Is Jane then more moral than God? Did my life become ruined simply because God was a bad landlord? What about in the "view" of cosmic morality? Who's a better person?

From my viewpoint, the entire "God as a borrower" scenario is flawed. I've blended ideas which I dare not consider in unison simply because I have God-beliefs. I've requested an answer to one question—Should I lend to God?—and put my own sense of cosmic morality under duress. The correct answer for one who believes in the superhuman presence of God is: Lend the dang money! The better answer for one who doesn't believe is: Never lend to any entity, deity or not, who's not likely to repay.

Regardless of personal belief, a lender must have some sort of faith or trust that a debt is likely to be repaid. The lender shall expect compensation for their participation in the transaction. The expectation is further confirmation that the transaction is the codification of a meta idea. Codification of a faith in repayment seems to move an instrument of debt from the realm of meta to the physical realm via a contract arrangement.

Debt, a contract for repayment, can be exchanged, swapped, or exchanged for value just like a tangible form of money. Nevertheless, debt itself hadn't commonly been thought of as an investment until very recently. Regardless, this is its principal use today. Debt exists not so much to finance a purchase but to create a kind of alternative money. Yes, common folk like you and I use debt to finance a car, a home, or even as a means to capitalize our businesses, but the major players of the world primarily use debt as an investment. The sad result is, debt, used in this way, has literally broken our traditional economic model.

We know the model is broken simply by looking at interest rates. It's obvious the debt isn't needed to facilitate capitalism simply because the interest rate on the debt is crazy low. No wise investor would lend a million dollars at an interest rate of, say, 2.5% for thirty years! Yet that is exactly what governments are doing. In fact, as of June 2019, the country of Austria managed to sell 98-year bonds which paid a rate of 1.17%! Who probably bought most of them? The same folks who lent the money.

The prime example of the irrelevance of debt has been the country of Greece, starting in 2009. Greece can't, hasn't, and won't pay its debts to the European Union. But there was no benefit to the EU to force collection. German and U.S. bankers couldn't repossess the country of Greece. What would the EU do after forcing debt collection? It could do absolutely nothing. Therefore, what the EU did, led by major global banking institutions, is simply extend the terms of the loans. Today the restructured payments are still not being made as scheduled, but the books show the debt is still valid. It's called the "extend and pretend strategy."

Extend and pretend works, at least for a while. The reason is the too big to fail dynamic and a shared currency. Banks and the EU member states can't let Greece fail without jeopardizing the reputation of France and Germany. Reputation and belief underpin the entire system. It is the single most important aspect of any money belief. These governments can afford to let you or I as individual homeowners fail, but if a country the size of Greece went bankrupt it would put the reputation of the EU at risk.

Citizens across the globe trust the EU, Japan, the USA, and alike. They may reconsider their impressions if or when they notice major bankruptcies. It's best for the system to pretend all's well. People have reflexively trusted the global economic system and have granted power to the governments that run the game. If it seems to work, we prefer not to think much about it. People in the U.S. don't know of this truth of money, but the greenback is also a shared currency. The U.S. dollar, the global reserve, is a currency shared in major bank and commodity markets. A collapse in the dollar, slow or fast, will result in a collapse in global banking and petroleum markets. There is little doubt about this result.

Major economies of the world, with the U.S. leading the pack, have accepted the idea that creating more money will keep individuals playing the game of economics. We will produce, spend, and consume; that is our game, our global hobby. And they're right. The majority of the world's population will continue to play their game as long as trust in the system remains. Their trust is exemplified by their continued acceptance of more debt and more money printing. Still, they won't play so quietly for more than another decade or so.

The most economically privileged subset of U.S. consumers, baby boomers, are slowly dying off and will die off en masse very soon. As this happens, the world's number one consumer and facilitator of the entire global model will be replaced by other consumers whose dominant mind-myths about money are different than that of the boomers. Societal opinions of money, wealth, value, and the U.S. fiat dollar will change, urging fundamental changes to the model itself. This period of transition will create doubts in market participants as they observe the world's economic system being in a state of flux. Fundamental trust in the system itself will be reconsidered. All bets will be off in times of systemic change.

CHAPTER 8

# A MYTH OF BEING EXPATRIATED

My comments about different types of governments, societal beliefs, and the potential of economic disruption might have started you thinking along a new line. Should you consider leaving the United States of America permanently? Out of curiosity and a hint of frustration, I've explored this question of expatriation (formally and legally forfeiting citizen rights) from the U.S. in some depth. I've decided that unless a person really hates this country or has for whatever reason deep loyalty to a new land, leaving the U.S. really isn't a practical option.

Regardless of my own conclusion, you may still be pondering the concept. I debated about putting this section in the book, but I'm asked about the topic at least a couple of times a year, so I thought I'd address a few basics. Any detailed discussion is beyond this book simply because I am not an attorney. Naturally, nothing presented here is to be considered legal advice.

Maybe you, like millions of other citizens, are so disenfranchised you believe you must make a change and truly find a new country. We want to belong within a society of like-minded thinkers, and those thinkers might be sitting in a different country than you are. A sense of belonging is an idea that most cherish. We are social animals and seem to need group membership to one degree or another. Government offers us protection, stability, and specific services. In an ideal world, our beliefs and values are in simpatico with our own government.

The depth, control, and structure of government today is relatively new. Today most citizens of modern governments exist under a sophisticated system that seemingly desires to micromanage its people by taxing, regulating, and monitoring almost every aspect of their existence. We can thank computer technology for facilitating this truth of modern society. Ancient Rome certainly had a somewhat sophisticated system of government 2000 years ago, and ancient Egypt 2000 years before Rome, but these, in terms of control and monitoring, are a joke compared to our own.

With that background, I guess it should be no wonder that millions of Americans ponder the idea of expatriation from a seemingly oppressive or simply undesirable country. People in the United States are oriented toward an appreciation of personal liberty. This truth is written into our very constitution. So when we observe government actions that seem to conflict with this fundamental premise, people are primed to eventually wonder, "Can I actually leave this country for another?"

The word expatriation refers to a legal process: the process of leaving your country in order to become a citizen in another. Does this sound like it would be no big deal? After all, from what we see on the news it appears thousands of people do it monthly. The southern border of the United States has seen over 100,000 unauthorized border crossings in one year. Aren't many of these people choosing to leave their country to establish citizenship in the United States? Yes, but taking up residence in another country doesn't mean that residency was approved by the country a person left.

Pursuant to the U.S. Department of State, expatriation done correctly requires government cooperation, taxation, and formal removal from citizenship roles. The United States government, technically the Internal Revenue Service (IRS), runs a very tight ship and doesn't make it easy to leave the good ole USA. Most of the regulations fall under the Foreign Account Tax Compliance Act (FATCA) and involve both the IRS and FBI. The government publishes a list of people who've successfully found their way through the maze of regulations quarterly. For the calendar quarter ended June 30, 2019, there were merely 609 names on that list. This small number of people were officially granted permission to leave for good. The listing contains the name of each individual losing United States citizenship (within the meaning of IRC 877A) with respect to whom the Secretary received information during the quarter ending June 30, 2019. For purposes of the listing, long-term residents, as defined in section 877(e)(2), will henceforth be treated as if they were citizens of the United States who lost citizenship.

How many are in the queue to become former citizens? How many thought they complied with all rules and failed? That information is not readily available. The process is difficult, and I suspect a number of people are well on their way to becoming an expatriated former citizen but have somehow gotten bogged down in the process.

Let me state this in bold: I AM NOT GIVING ANY FORM OF LEGAL ADVICE IN THIS BOOK. I SPECIFICALLY INSTRUCT, NOT RECOMMEND, THAT YOU SEEK ADVICE OF AN ATTORNEY SHOULD YOU WISH TO HAVE ANY SERIOUS DISCUSSION ABOUT EXPATRIATION. ANY INFORMATION IS PRESENTED AS A CASUAL AND INFORMAL DISCUSSION FOR ENTERTAINMENT PURPOSES ONLY. With that said, let me list a few things, steps if you will, that might be considered before electing to become expatriated.

1. Move to the other country and seek to obtain citizenship. You must have a country willing to accept your presence. Expatriation must be done from the new country.

2. Once you've obtained your new citizenship and are working with an experienced attorney, you can move forward to voluntarily relinquish U.S. citizenship as follows:

    A. Appear in person before a U.S. consul or diplomatic officer. This is done in a foreign country at a U.S. Embassy or consulate.

    B. You will then sign an oath of renunciation.

3. Each renouncing citizen will need to present an accounting in order to calculate an "exit tax," technically known as an expatriation tax or emigration tax. Conceptually, this works similar to an estate tax. Included in the presentation are a minimum of five years of tax returns (which will be audited) and a fee of about $2,500. The tax rate is roughly 25–30% of the value over the tax-free base. The good news is the tax-free base is quite high. The bad news is it's calculated based upon your global assets, not simply those domiciled in the USA. This will include the value of your residence and retirement accounts.

4. Persons intending to renounce should be aware that they may be rendered stateless and lack the protection of any government. They may have difficulty traveling, obtaining a passport, visa, work, or own or rent property as a result.

5. Renunciation may have no effect on their U.S. tax or military obligations.

6. Parents may not renounce the citizenship of a minor child.

7. Renunciation is irrevocable and cannot be canceled or set aside absent successful judicial or administrative appeal.

Expatriation has serious consequences, and for those reasons, most who consider the idea choose a less drastic alternative; they live abroad while retaining U.S. citizenship. These people are often called *expats,* but as you know, living abroad is not the same as actually giving up citizenship. An expat could simply be a person who takes a regular but long vacation outside of the U.S. The exact figures are very difficult to calculate, but it is estimated that roughly nine to ten million Americans are taking an extended vacation, living in a second home, or simply living abroad at any particular time. Forty percent of those remain in the Western hemisphere—Canada, South, and Central America—with another 25% or so in Europe. Ecuador is a favorite hangout of expats.

Living abroad isn't simply a matter of renting a house in an exotic location like Costa Rica or Paris. Healthcare for a person from the U.S. can be tricky whether it's needed by an expat, holiday traveler, or expatriated citizen. Most countries that Americans go to have some form of nationalized healthcare, but these typically don't cover persons other than permanent residents. For the most part, your U.S health insurance won't be accepted in payment, and Medicare rarely pays for care abroad. For this reason, several U.S. based insurance companies do offer policies that insure people abroad. If you or someone you care for plans on being outside of the United States for an extended period of time, it is imperative that they understand the healthcare available in their location.

W. Durwood Johnson

Getting a job in a foreign land can be done in most cases even without formal renunciation of citizenship. Still, foreign countries frequently limit the amount of income a foreigner can earn or even the number of hours they may work. Some areas of the globe have exceedingly high unemployment rates; consequently, these governments want to make sure foreigners aren't taking jobs from residents. Violation of local standards and laws could result in substantial fines and/or incarceration.

The U.S. government generally doesn't care where income is earned or how it's legally received as long as it's reported and taxed appropriately by interested governments. The U.S. is the only industrialized government that requires its citizens to pay tax on their worldwide income, therefore income earned abroad can be subject to double-taxation. Failure to pay tax obligations may be interpreted as a criminal act by the IRS.

Retaining money, investments, or business interest in locations outside of the U.S. is an issue that piques the interest of the government. A United States citizen, in most cases, can have investments domiciled in a foreign country provided you retain a full history of the source of the value and report said amount annually. As with most things involving the IRS, disclosure is the key to staying in their good graces.

I want to briefly address what is commonly referred to as "dual citizenship." I occasionally meet clients who inform me they are dual citizens of both the U.S. and wherever. Some people have or get passports from other countries. They then refer to themselves as being dual citizens, when in fact this second passport doesn't mean much of anything from a legal standpoint. Since the U.S. doesn't legally recognize a dual citizen status, its citizens can't legally be dual citizens despite their personal paperwork. It's often reported that U.S. law does not mention dual nationality or require a person to choose one nationality over another. However, from a practical standpoint, it seems to me that once you're wholly bound as a U.S. citizen, swearing allegiance, any other status you've had becomes irrelevant from the standpoint of the federal government.

A principal reason that people contemplate renouncing their U.S. citizenship seems to be the Internal Revenue Code (code). We in the U.S. are taxed on our global income. This is no big deal for the vast majority; however, if you had substantial investments in other lands you'd probably feel differently. You might even consider giving up your citizenship simply to minimize your own personal income tax burden.

CHAPTER 9

# TAXES AND A VOLUNTARY MYTH

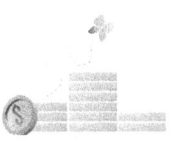

Let me begin by saying I won't be at all technical in this chapter. I want to give you some sense of the U.S. tax system from the view of one who deals with it almost every working day. I respect the system and believe I understand it's purpose. My hope is by exposing my own understanding or myth of interpretation you can better enlighten your own. If the very idea of taxes causes anxiety, you may possibly start to appreciate that while your fear is real, it's rather unnecessary.

Globally speaking, our tax system is unique. The U.S. system causes our citizens to be taxed on their global income, not simply that derived from this country. This serves to prevent citizens from setting up profit centers outside the country for fear of double-taxation. Often a tax credit is available to mitigate the problem, but this credit varies from country to country. I want to pause to highlight an underlying idea rooted in U.S. theory. In short, the government owns its citizens.

Recall our discussion of philosophy and specifically the ideas of Adam Smith. He wrote of his Ultrathought that the value of a country was locked within the value of its citizens. The U.S. tax system subscribes to this idea to a tee. Citizens are the worth of the U.S.; therefore, the federal government can't simply allow its people, its value, to go abroad and earn money without payment of toll to the government. In theory, we don't simply live on this land—we're a resource owned by the country. We are its value just as Smith described in his concepts, and many of our laws, particularly income tax laws, are written with this theory in mind. Understanding the history of this myth and how our constitution incorporates the premise can make dealing with taxation much easier, at least conceptually.

Another peculiarity of our system is its reliance on the concept of "voluntary" compliance. Most countries force tax compliance, and while the IRS is an enforcement agency, our government theoretically gives us the benefit of the doubt. Keeping Adam Smith and his predecessor John Locke in mind, you'll note that our system allows us a certain liberty to not comply simply because technically the whole system is voluntary. Our laws assume people are innately moral and will comply with authority. That myth can be sourced to thinkers of the $15^{th}$, $16^{th}$, and $17^{th}$ centuries.

On the contrary, other countries seem to assume the worst in people. They will go so far as to literally issue government cash registers complete with monitoring devices to assure merchants pay tax. They collect tax not annually but right there at the point of each transaction. Now maybe you understand why bazaars are so popular in certain countries. Often these facilitate black market or off-the-books sales which aren't taxed by their governments. The U.S. is different. Here the government doesn't believe it needs to authorize things like cash registers. The government's operating assumption is that merchants will be honest. Most of the time its trust is justified. With that said, the IRS does own 4,487 guns including 621 shotguns and 15 submachine guns as of 2017. Enforcement of tax law will be accomplished one way or another.

People and merchants are assumed to fulfill their tax obligations voluntarily at least once a year. Each citizen and entity shall file a disclosure form complete with a calculation of self-assessed tax. Implied in the statement is the idea that a citizen could simply elect *not* to comply. That would be a grave misunderstanding. While no taxpayer is expected to be an expert in taxation, each is required to comply with the law, and the law requires the filing of a valid form. Voluntary incrimination might be a better way to think of it.

The issue of whether one's compliance is required or voluntary has been litigated in various ways over the decades. There have been some lucid theories posed in hopes of justifying a person's right to choose not to voluntarily comply. Citizens have cited constitutional arguments supported by the 5th, 13th, and 16th amendments. Still, all of the important cases have been settled. The highest courts in the country have repeatedly determined that the U.S. Constitution grants authority to the agency known as the Internal Revenue Service (IRS) to enforce tax laws, the filing of forms, and to collect several types of tax through various means. So, in summary, we might paraphrase: The system is *voluntary* to the extent that in good faith taxpayers must self-assess and pay a tax. The IRS, at its sole discretion, can refigure the taxpayer's original calculations pursuant to the U.S. Tax Code forcing collection, penalties, and interest on any amount unpaid. That's the law, period.

The Internal Revenue Code is a specific set of laws dealing with various forms of federal tax. We most commonly think of income tax, but the tax code actually deals with several different types of federal tax. Regarding income tax, within these laws the default position of the code is that virtually any receipt of value is assumed to be income. That income is subject to tax by default. The code then softens its default stance by allowing certain *exclusions* of income, *deductions* from income, and *exemptions* of certain types of income from income tax.

What are these exclusions, deductions, and exempt income items? In a raw sense, they are the actual "'loopholes'" you so often hear about. These provisions are either built into the code or come as a direct result of court cases and certain interpretations by the IRS. What's commonly called a loophole are the details of the legislation which determines the final calculation of income, gift, estate, and other matters of U.S. taxation. A loophole is neither good nor bad; it's simply a fundamental part of the tax law.

Common loopholes used by millions of taxpayers deal with money given to charity and mortgage interest paid on a principal residence. Tax code informs individual taxpayers that they can, in certain cases, deduct from taxable income amounts paid to authorized charitable institutions and interest paid regarding certain types of secured debt. This is neither good nor bad. It is simply the law.

A basic understanding of income taxes and so-called tax loopholes can ease your stress about income taxes, but *understanding* won't make you happy. In fact, if you actually read the tax code you'll probably get more frustrated than less. The tax code is filled with tortured language much of which seems to be written in an attempt to camouflage some nuance of the law which benefits some company somewhere. No amount of carping by you or I will change tax law, so frankly I think complaining about income taxes is akin to complaining about the weather. Why bother?

In my view, we'd all be happier if we could internalize this one absolute truth about U.S. tax law. *The code is not fair, and it was never intended to be.* What tax laws are is fair enough to keep citizens from rioting in the streets. Taxes exist to guide citizen behavior, redistribute wealth, and support the objectives of the government. The IRS is simply doing what the agency is asked to do: collect taxes assessed and encourage citizen compliance.

Congress created the metaphorical cards called the code and the IRS holds all of them. The law is on their side. The IRS doesn't want to create problems for citizens of the United States. The IRS, at the behest of our government, simply wants citizens to accurately assess and pay any tax due. If a citizen makes a good faith effort to comply with the rules, generally speaking, all will go well. If, on the other hand, the citizen simply ignores his or her obligation to voluntarily comply, the U.S. Department of the Treasury will force compliance. In my experience, perfection is not required—simply diligence and good faith.

Don't write me. I am not an agent of the government. What I am is candid. The IRS isn't evil nor are they fair. Fairness is purely a meta concept. You can't measure what is fair. What is a fair tax to you may be patently offensive to me. Fairness is an extremely ill-defined and contextual term. It can't and will never be codified into law to the satisfaction of all. Therefore, we shouldn't react negatively to a loophole or tax code interpretation that goes against us. What you should do is elect U.S. government representatives who share your vision for the country. Representatives dictate tax law, not the IRS.

As you probably know, home mortgage interest can be deducted from your taxable income while rent paid is not deductible. This is a loophole in favor of homeowners who take on mortgage debt. Like most of tax law, this provision has evolved over time. Tax laws aren't constant, which is one of the reasons that long-term financial planning is so difficult. For instance, did you know it is entirely possible that at some point Congress might simply decide to tax you on your accumulated balances within your retirement accounts, even though you haven't yet taken any distributions? This has recently been voted down in a congressional committee, but watch for the provision in the coming years. Taxes are one of the certainties of life, but the details of exactly how that is applied in practice are far from certain.

The history of the mortgage loophole is illustrative of the way things evolve within provisions of tax law. The U.S. Congress first decided it would be good to encourage citizens to take on debt at the dawn of tax law roughly one hundred years ago. They undoubtedly noticed that if they could encourage businesses to borrow they frequently used this capital to purchase equipment or products. This, in turn, stimulated economic growth. At that time, they only allowed the loophole to be used by businesses, but eventually, Congress expanded the law to include all consumer debt. Auto loan, credit card, mortgage, and business debt—it made no difference. Interest paid was allowed to be deducted from your income in computing your taxable income.

The reason they first expanded the loophole beyond businesses was because the IRS couldn't efficiently categorize interest expense paid by the millions of small businesses. Large corporations could take on legitimate business debt, but small business owners were often forced to use consumer loans to finance their business expansion. This meant small companies were at a disadvantage to the giants. So, in time, Congress changed the law to allow all interest paid to be deducted.

The law has changed several times, and in some years people could deduct things like credit card and auto loan interest, and in other years they couldn't. Tax law can never be assumed stable. In 1986, a major change occurred with regard to interest deductions. Congress decided to restrict the deduction of non-business interest almost entirely with one major exception. The tax loophole remained in regard to interest paid on a primary home mortgage plus that of a second home, both being subject to a limit. This change was made to offset tax rate reductions provided in the *Tax Reform Act of 1986*. The government needed more tax money from citizens.

The home mortgage interest loophole seems to be a favorite subject for Congress. This is mostly because massive amounts of tax can be shifted with one rather basic change but also because home construction is a major industry in the United States. When Congress moves tax money, it also moves the economy. Though given the exceedingly low interest rates of today, it's debatable whether any future change will do the same. The law most recently changed in the *Tax Cuts and Jobs Act of 2017*. In that change, only mortgage interest paid on up to $750,000 worth of debt remains deductible.

Tax minimization is allowed, if not encouraged, by using loopholes built into tax law, but ignoring your tax-related obligations or evading tax can be a serious crime. The informed taxpayer understands the difference between taking advantage of the code and evading tax altogether. If you're ever unfortunate enough to get a letter from the IRS, they're simply telling you they need more information. Do yourself a favor; answer their letter within the time frame stated. If necessary, explain in-depth with attachments. Regardless, say something.

If you get a letter, whatever you do, don't ignore the letter or pretend you never received it. This won't work. The IRS won't get tired of sending letters, and pursuant to law, if they don't hear from you they may levy your assets. Yes, it is possible that the IRS could lose track of you temporarily, but ultimately when you get your social security check, they'll sync up the databases. The IRS is like the cyborg in *The Terminator* movie. They just keep coming and won't stop. However, like Arnold, the IRS is rational. They have their program, but if you understand what their goal is, you can very often work with them to resolve any issues in less than a year.

Of course, my myths of belief with regard to the IRS are my own. Other professionals disagree; they don't think of the IRS as the terminator. To some of my colleagues, the IRS is viewed more as an opponent who's involved in a three-year game of chess. Naturally, these professionals choose to be obstinate in dealing with the IRS. Admittedly, I've been both pleased and surprised that through diligence, tax research, and even a hint of obstinance, well-seasoned professionals can manage to survive or even occasionally win against the IRS. While I still prefer my strategy—follow the rules to begin with—I respect that not everyone is so motivated.

I'm what you might call "drama averse." Others might be characterized as being "drama seeking." People vary in temperament. So, if you ever find yourself in an IRS jam, stop. Ask yourself, do you seek drama or not? If you handle it well, you may be rewarded by fighting the feds. If not, your whole IRS issue will go away more painlessly if you simply work with them.

We are extremely fortunate to live in the United States. Being a representative republic, given enough time, our federal government is generally responsive to the desires of its citizens. There are always exceptions, but I can tell you that in my three-plus decades dealing with the IRS and federal income tax reporting, most of the issues come as a direct result of people not acting in good faith. The number one reason people have problems is they fail to file forms, period. I'm not speaking of not filing them correctly, I'm saying not filing at all.

The way the IRS works, if forms aren't filed they simply assume *everything* is income and no deductions of consequence exist. Their assumption is incorrect in all but a handful of cases; still, absent any information, this is what they'll assume. If need be, they will even complete your "voluntary" forms for you. Unfortunately, they'll assume things play out in their favor. Can you appeal and correct the record? Yes, within the provisions of the law. However, if you ignore the law or misinterpret provisions, you may leave the IRS no choice but to force collection. They will find your assets and take, levy, or lien them as payment of mandatory taxes. They will do so because we as citizens have ceded control and granted power to this agency of our society.

CHAPTER 10

# THE MYTH OF RETIREMENT

The broad idea of retirement is a relatively new myth only recently accepted by humanity. People just a hundred years ago didn't obsess about how they would have enough money for the final two decades of their lives. Though the idea started decades before in Europe, the American concept of retirement changed drastically in the U.S. with the invention of our social security or government-sponsored workers' pension system in 1935. The idea is rooted in a collectivist ideology: It's best for society overall to retire older workers to make way for younger workers who can be more productive. Greater productivity benefits the group regardless of its impact on the individual. To soften the individual impact, the government shall provide a minimal pension to offset the loss of wage income. Prior to this time, common folks typically worked until they couldn't.

Today most of us ponder the idea of retirement, and a growing number seem to consider it more like an obligation than an election. Retirement has become an important concept in and of itself apart from the myth of money. We've created several ancillary myths associated with this idea. We assume we're owed this "benefit" of becoming irrelevant. Given we tend to think of retirement as a benefit rather than a curse of old age, we look forward to receiving some subsistence level of income for the rest of our lives.

Many of us seem to view the concept as a kind of law of the land. Some people literally obsess about retirement or its funding. With that, it's safe to assume that this idea has a great deal to do with the personal happiness of thousands if not millions of people. Unfortunately, many of these ideas are reflexive opinions or worse. Some people have created opinions about retirement that are rather ill-conceived.

Let's begin by setting your own narrative on a path to enlightenment with two brief declarations. First, retirement is a choice, not an obligation. Second, retirement shortens your life.

Remember, you are in control. Retirement is just another idea, and it's certainly not the law. Yes, your boss or firm might urge you to retire for whatever reason; however, it is actually rather difficult to force retirement. There are exceptions. Airline pilots are forced to retire, for instance, but even this long-time policy is likely to be changed in the coming years. Regarding the government, we're not living in the 1930s. The unemployment rate is low, so the U.S. government prefers that you stay employed. They want your tax dollars and understand that you are a valuable asset to this country.

Being in control of when or if you retire, it's important for you to appreciate that a job that is meaningful to you, regardless of the compensation level, is likely to help you emotionally. As a result, that job may be worth keeping even if you were to work for free! When you're employed, being consistently engaged in something, you will stay healthier and live longer. Longevity is correlated with your feelings of self-worth just as it is with physical exercise.

If you subscribe to the belief that you should retire, you really need to seriously think through the details several years before its theoretical date. Maybe you should attempt to live on what you believe you'd have available each month for a full six months some years before your idea of a retirement date. Think of it as an extended vacation. Heck, tell your employer it's a medical issue. With some luck, maybe they won't ask too many questions. While on this sabbatical, go beyond the financial aspects of retirement and consider what you would actually do for ten, twenty, or thirty years. This decision will be one of the most important decisions of your life. Don't simply follow the crowd. Ultra-think!

As people approach retirement, a strategy I've recommended to at least a hundred people over the years is to compromise your personal work ethic. You heard that right. Become a sub-par employee doing just barely enough to stay employed. Literally, I tell my clients who say they plan on retiring tomorrow to "Retire on the job and wait for your boss to figure it out!" Most people actually won't or simply can't, but a dozen or more people who have taken my advice have been extremely happy they did. None have ever told me they regretted becoming a slacker.

To ease your mind about becoming that *worthless* employee, sort of retiring on the job, let me remind you—the decision to keep you employed is ultimately your employer's. They can and should act in their best interests. Yes, small businesses can be different, and I know I do care about my staff like family. If one of my staff retired on the job, I'd notice—and we'd have a heart-to-heart discussion hoping to mutually resolve their issue. Still, a big faceless corporation really doesn't care about you. I understand my words are harsh, but in my experience they are true. Any firm which is engaged in commerce for profit should, and most will, act in their own best interest. I suggest you do the same.

Your employer is not your best friend and doesn't care about you more than the entity. Your employer is simply a party to a contract, written or implied. A contract, by the way, that the employer has penned. Furthermore, if the employer violates the law in any way forcing retirement upon you in a manner which is suspect, make noise. Sue if necessary, letting the law run its course. Manage your career as a business because you can rest assured your employer does.

One reason it is so satisfying to become the slacker employee for as long as you can is that it reminds you that you're in charge. Sure, maybe you end up getting fired, but so what? You asked for it. Change your own myth about employment in general. Be the deadwood employee you've always bad-mouthed! Maybe you'll even be able to collect unemployment after being shown the door.

I urge you to consider your retirement funding from a fair mind well before you retire. I'll be very blunt here. Unless you have a very high pension or social security payment coming to you, your home is paid off, you have at least $100,000 in the bank, you're in very good health, and you simply don't spend much money, you really should accept the fact that you will need to live quite frugally in retirement. For most, a social security pension payment won't support their current lifestyle.

Can you live on your social security if you have no mortgage or a very low rent obligation? Let me put you at ease. Yes, in most parts of this country you can live on social security as long as that figure exceeds $1800–$2200 per month. True, your necessary lifestyle probably wouldn't be ideal, but you won't starve. Assuming you have a house payment or are required to pay rent in excess of roughly $900 per month per person, I believe you'd need a social security payment in excess of $2700 per month to live. If you insist on living in high-cost areas, obviously this amount of regular money coming in won't be enough for even the most meager standard of living.

Assuming an ultra-low standard of living, people can live on very little money largely because we're a generous nation. We Americans tend to take care of our citizens whether it's through charity or government assistance. When we observe others in what appears to be financial distress, we're unsettled ourselves. To release our own angst, we provide charity and demand that our government steps in to help. In theory, aid given will subsidize a person's standard of living through their crisis. Assistance will also tacitly urge people to abandon their alternative arrangements and join the rest of us "normal" citizens. Society has a myth about lifestyle, and living on the street or "van down by the river" isn't in it in the United States.

Our societal myth regarding lifestyle tends to assume everyone in America will eventually aspire to obtain the same lifestyle promoted in consumer advertisements. Naturally, this won't happen; still, it is an underlying assumption of our Western culture. This misunderstanding is part of the reason our politicians aren't able to effectively manage problems like homelessness. They don't appreciate that people have a divergent set of truths, desires, and values. Leaders assume everybody wants a stable home, most likely in the suburbs, and no one really wants to live in a tent on a sidewalk in a city like San Francisco. Our leaders are wrong.

Some people, certainly not most, view camping as a viable living alternative for one who has very little money. Don't make the mistake of politicians and confuse elective camping with true homelessness. These are entirely different circumstances. Homelessness demands attention and may involve things like economic, social, medical, or substance rehabilitation services. Urban campers need little more than low-cost campsites.

Assuming an individual is willing to accept a very low standard of living and all the drama associated with rogue camping, they could save a minimum of $700 to $1500 per month by camping. This site could be set up on a sidewalk, park, shoreline, land easement, or freeway underpass. That individual could then establish a PO Box and a bank account. He or she would then have any social security payments directly deposited and pay typical bills like anyone else. They'd then quite easily live without any static address. What would be their cost of living? I think an urban camper could live on less than $1,000 a month. It's all about lifestyle. I further believe we are at the forefront of a rapidly growing trend. Many thousands of folks who choose to retire will simply elect to camp rather than formally rent a residence.

Naturally, most who read books like this don't believe setting up a rogue campsite is a worthy retirement living suggestion. We sort of buy into the idea that normal life in the U.S. includes owning or renting a rather permanent address, so we'll set the camping idea aside for the moment. Let's ponder the typical retirement. In my experience there seem to be five keys to creating what most would call an adequate retirement experience.

- Work enough to push your social security payment toward its maximum payout. Usually, you need twenty to thirty years earning at least an average wage. Note, social security calculations currently consider your highest thirty-five years of employment earnings.

- Pay off your low tax and low maintenance home in an affordable area within five years of retirement.

- Save at least $250,000 per household member within a diversified investment portfolio.

- Seek to maintain good overall health, and live in an area with adequate healthcare services.

- Work a part-time job or create obligations which demand your attention (i.e., commit to volunteerism, club participation, babysitting, mentoring, etc.).

Do each of these five, and in my estimation, you'll have a fulfilling and adequately funded retirement. You'll note I did not discuss retirement age because this is dependent upon each of the five other considerations. While these five are the keys, there are other issues for you to consider. Most you've heard, but still, they're worth repeating.

If you have an opportunity to invest through work in some sort of retirement fund, you really should participate. These accounts offer immediate tax savings. However, don't participate unless you have a safety net of cash reserves equal to at least one, preferably three months cash need on hand, and you have quality health insurance. In order of importance, most people's financial priorities should be having a safety net, healthcare insurance, retirement fund, and then manageable consumer debt. Debt repayment is fourth because in my experience I often find people simply pay off debt to run the number back up cyclically. It's unfortunate, and frankly it makes no sense, but I see this all of the time.

Regarding investing for retirement, what percentage of your pay, or how much to put per year into the company-sponsored plan, I suggest the following: The minimum amount of your savings should be the amount of the employer match. The maximum amount is an individual choice, but don't kid yourself. If you are only putting aside a few thousand dollars per year, you will probably find you've significantly underfunded your retirement. Do the math—$5,000 per year for twenty years would probably be worth, assuming some typical rate of return, about $125,000 to $200,000 in twenty years. What would $150,000 mean in retirement? Not near as much as you'd think given the typical retired person spends 15–20 years in retirement. You need to fund a bunch to have a bunch. If you fund less than about $10,000 per year for any less than twenty years, in my experience you won't accumulate what I'd call "enough" to make any real difference in your net worth.

The issue of when to elect to take social security is a subject of nuance. Believe it or not, most people take social security before they reach full social security retirement age. In doing so they may be cutting the value of their check by twenty-five percent. This, in my view, is usually a mistake, so I rarely recommend it. Regardless of my own view, everyone really should ultra-think the topic before making their own decisions about social security. Furthermore, I urge you to sit down with a social security advisor. Have them show you all of the variables. Remove emotion, suppress all of your own so-thought "logical" assumptions about social security, and get all the facts from people who understand the system.

There is no absolute formula to make a determination, but there are certain rules of thumb. With that said, I'll share my views about when and when not to turn on your own social security pension stream in retirement.

- If you've done all you can to cut your discretionary spending and you still simply can't live within your current income, take social security. I won't preach, but you can probably guess what my sermon would be. I'll leave it there.

- If you're not expected to live to normal life expectancy due to cancer, heart failure, smoking with a history of cancer, obesity, or have a poor family health history, take social security sooner rather than later.
- If you have very little money in savings, probably take social security sooner rather than later. Remember, my number one recommendation is to build a safety net of cash reserves. This common-sense advice becomes an urgent recommendation when you're older.
- If you are in very good health and longevity runs in your family, mathematically the odds suggest you should delay taking social security until the monthly amount stops increasing. Under current law that is age seventy.
- Finally, don't take social security until age seventy if you or your spouse still works unless you are in poor health. Earned income often causes your social security to be subject to income tax. Therefore, if you're still earning an income, any money you receive from the government will be taxed. What that means is you'll only keep about 70–90% of whatever money you get from social security after taxes are considered.

I'm often asked what some would assume would be a rather easy question for a CPA or CFP®: "How much do I need to retire?" I have only one answer: "No one can tell you how much is 'enough' to retire." Even if one can tell me precisely what their lifestyle would be, I can't answer this question correctly because neither inflation nor investment performance is predictable in the long run. So absolutely no one can precisely predict their ultimate financial needs.

Sure, we can make some assumptions. Unfortunately, the assumptions are rather meaningless beyond ten years. Any small variance actually experienced will drastically skew future values exponentially. Regardless, even if somehow we stumbled upon the correct assumptions about rate of return and inflation, reliably predicting much of anything else is pretty much impossible in the long run. Beyond ten years, life is a whole lot of mystery in regard to health, person, state, insurance costs, family issues, and taxation. Retirement planning, therefore, becomes as much of a gut feeling as a mathematical calculation.

Since predictions of life and economics beyond ten years are basically crapshoots, does this mean we shouldn't plan? Of course not. There are certainly things you can and should do if having a happy retirement experience is your goal.

Statistics inform us there are some rather predictable destroyers of a happy retirement, and while money issues are most often pointed to it is poor overall health, not money, which wrecks retirement for most. Hearing loss, knee problems, shortness of breath—these are the things that make living so difficult in old age. The irony is, solutions to these issues are often within your grasp. You must do whatever you can to get yourself healthier before the age of sixty. Most people can remain vibrant into their eighties but only if they stay ahead of health challenges.

Having a healthcare advocate is important today and may be required in the future. As our healthcare system evolves, though it will be technologically personalized, it will become extremely impersonal. Without an advocate on your side, you will risk being lost in the system; just another number in an overcrowded hospital in times of crisis. If you don't have children or you can't rely on your children to be your care advocate, you really need to purchase a long-term care policy if you can afford it. I suggest you do so, not because it is a wise financial choice (though it often is) but for the care management aspect. In the coming decade it will become quite evident that if you don't have an advocate for your care you will not get quality care.

Reckless spending is often a sign of deep-seated emotional problems, and reckless spending in retirement will probably lead to a troubling last few years of life. Most everyone has some level of money drama, and much of that baggage comes as a result of a lack of personal understanding. There have been a number of good books written which describe various personality profiles that lead to certain behaviors. I have no desire to rehash them. What is important is that you appreciate that the mind is dominant, and if you have certain tendencies that appear to run in conflict with your own stated objectives, you likely have a less than healthy relationship with money. Things won't get better in retirement, they'll get worse. Figure it out, and you'll be on your way to releasing your own stress with regards to money. As they say, "check yourself before you wreck yourself" financially.

Subsidizing their children's finances is a major reason that millions of retirees come up short in retirement. In my years as a consultant this one statement has made more clients angry at me than any other, despite the fact they know it needs to be said. Guilt-ridden baby boomers often seem to foist their own lifestyle choices on children who honestly couldn't care less. In doing so they urge their own children toward a lifestyle beyond their means. This creates stress in both the life of the child and the parent. The best thing you can do for your family is to take care of yourself. And the best thing you can do for your children is allowing them to fail and internalize their own life experiences. Absent unusual circumstances, say a mental handicap, that means cutting the kids off financially. Your resolve to say no to your children when they could use a bit of financial "help" benefits all concerned.

Consumer debt is fine, but excessive consumer debt puts a cap on your prospects for wealth accumulation. How much is too much? That is difficult to say; however, if you routinely can't afford to pay off your own credit card within about six months, you probably carry too much card debt. While credit card debt is probably the most annoying type of debt it may not be the worst type of consumer debt. Recurrent auto loans/leases often set people up for failure. Very few single items are as expensive as car leases. These are the biggest scam put upon a senior citizen who's struggling to make ends meet.

Being "house poor" is owning more house than you can afford. Remember that your neighborhood tends to anchor your lifestyle. If your neighbors make about $200,000 a year and you make about $60,000, you'll probably end up living beyond your means simply because the peer pressure of your neighbors urges you to spend more than you should. Furthermore, be advised that the true cost of homeownership should include a repair and maintenance savings account equal to roughly 3% of the home's value every year of ownership. This is often not considered by homeowners, which is why people are frequently put in financial distress by a rather predictable expense like a new HVAC system or roof. If you live in a $500,000 home, you'd then be expected to set aside about $15,000 a year for maintenance. Consequently, big old homes cost big bucks to maintain in retirement.

The neighborhood you currently live in may be incredible, but if you're no longer with your peer group you probably want to think about moving. If so, don't wait! You can't downsize too soon if you're over the age of seventy. To downsize means far more than simply reducing the square footage of your living space. If your goal is to truly downsize, ask yourself: Am I downsizing because the home is too big or because I need to free up some cash? For most, the answer will be a blend of both. Therefore, make sure you don't simply lose square footage only to replace that home with a similarly priced residence. Pick a neighborhood where your neighbors probably bring home less money than you will in retirement. Appreciate your goals, and stop justifying subpar solutions to rather easy challenges.

Failing to appreciate that at some point your mental ability will decline is a mistaken myth in my view. It seems to me that while we shouldn't look forward to the decline we shouldn't fear it either. Take steps to keep it healthy today and tomorrow, but when your mind or that of your loved one goes, hug it out and keep moving forward. What's certain in life? Death, taxes, and the fact that if you live long enough your mental acuity will noticeably decline. Yes, there are exceptions, but they are few and far between. Remember, someone will win the lottery tonight, but the millions who don't shouldn't plan on a jackpot. Whether you end up getting Alzheimer's disease or you simply become senile makes little difference. You need to plan for the certainty of a mental decline.

Finally, let me close my retirement discussion by urging you to accept the fact that your time on this planet is slipping away. Very few of us will stay vibrant beyond our mid-eighties, so plan for your own death before you're seventy or seventy-five. Yes, you may be wrong, but such visualization will help you let go of your life with dignity. Remember, everyone sort of has a last will and testament. Some of us write one, and others use the default will of the state they die in. To think with intent is to act with intent by writing down your last wishes in accordance with the law.

Whatever your concept of retirement is, I urge you to not reflexively buy into the common societal myth without ultra-thinking first. Retirement is simply one way to live as an elder, and it certainly isn't the best choice for everyone. Go out on your terms, having done some ultra-thinking about your final years on this planet: your purpose, your legacy, and most importantly the person you left in our societal memory. Yes, it was all a delusion you created, but it can be a delusion created with intent.

CHAPTER 11

# AN ELECTRIC PREDICTION

Since roughly 2013, I've been telling anyone who'll listen that it's time to get ready to face some big challenges between now and 2030. Several of these deal directly with economics, but before returning to a primary theme of this book I must address a rather different issue: our reliance on electricity distributed through an antiquated centralized system.

It seems rather obvious that our total reliance on electric power which is delivered via an interconnected electric grid poses the single greatest risk to our modern mechanized society. I am nearly certain that at some point millions of people in one or more urbanized areas will experience a power outage lasting weeks, months, or even years. My warning is not outlandish or even outside of mainstream opinion. FEMA (Federal Emergency Management Agency) agrees with me. The risk of a prolonged widespread power outage is extremely high.

The list of reasons for such a disruption is long. These include terrestrial events like hurricanes, earthquakes, and forest fires, but these concern me far less than the potential for some type of global electromagnetic event. Periods of unusual solar activity and seemingly rare supernova events happen far more often than people realize. A star explosion from hundreds if not thousands of light-years away could literally take civilization back to the Stone Age in a matter of months, and a rough period of solar activity could wreak havoc, disrupting the lives of billions. We must also be aware that man-caused electromagnetic disruption is not only possible, but it's also relatively easy to accomplish. EMP (electromagnetic pulse) weapons or overt sabotage of our electric grid could leave vast swaths of the planet without power for an uncertain period of time, depending upon the nature of the attack. A major power outage could even occur simply because of an innocent failure of an operator. Frankly, the reason for the outage won't be particularly important to the victims. They won't be able to Google it anyway because when the power goes, the internet will be rendered useless within hours.

Just try to imagine a quarter or even half of the country being without power. Sure, I'll probably be proven incorrect in assuming that this event is likely to occur in my own lifetime, but the way I see it, there's virtually no downside to being prepared. It's not difficult to maintain a couple of weeks of essentials on hand. Furthermore, taking the time to discuss some sort of get-out-of-town plan wastes, what, an hour? Basic preparedness is what I'm talking about. I'm not saying folks should prepare for a zombie apocalypse, but every citizen owes it to themselves, their family, and their country to be prepared to go a minimum of two weeks without electric power.

In this book, I won't say much else about this risk, but in Appendix 1 you will find a reprint of my own "Get Ready" prep list. Use mine or create your own; either way, get ready for a power failure! The risk is real, and preparation, at least that necessary for a couple of weeks of survival, isn't all that difficult. Though I am no soothsayer, I won't be wrong in predicting this event. Nevertheless, I may be early. Regardless, I'd rather be early than be caught unprepared.

My personal confidence that there will be a widescale power outage largely rests on statistics. Of all my predictions, this is the one I'm most confident in making. My confidence is bolstered by learned assessments by folks very well versed in the subject. FEMA, the Congressional Committee on Energy and Commerce, and the National Aeronautics and Space Administration (NASA) shout the same message: Get ready!

CHAPTER 12

# A MYTH OF SOLVENCY

It is undeniable that there has been far more debt issued than will ever be paid back. The global economic system functions today, and some believe it will continue to do so for decades to come, if for no other reason than all major economic powers are in the same boat. As the theory goes, no sovereign nation of consequence will dare rock the boat by questioning the wisdom of continuing to loan money based on a fantasy that it will ever be repaid. I suggest that after a bit of ultra-thinking you'll put this myth in its own context. The theory is one thing, but our own financial best interests aren't theoretical. We should take necessary steps now to save ourselves before the "smart folks" push us so far out to sea that we can't swim to shore.

In my humble opinion, I believe the whole global economic system could begin to show overt signs of failure at any time. Just like when an overloaded lifeboat flips, once one of the few biggest economies fail (United States, China, Japan, European Union, United Kingdom, India), they'll all fail in less than twenty-four months. Yes, it is that bad. Governments will scramble and solutions will eventually be found, but for a period of time citizens will be on their own, and some won't financially survive. With a bit of forethought, I suggest we can increase our own odds of financial survival.

I won't bore you with actual crazy numbers—the multiple trillions of dollars of debt. Google it if you need that type of detail. Frankly, the actual figures vary and wouldn't mean anything to you anyway. The human mind can't comprehend tens of trillions of dollars. By the way, did you know $66 trillion stacked in dollar bills would stretch roughly 4.5 million miles?! That's about eighteen times the distance between the earth and the moon. Put succinctly, the amount of sovereign debt exceeds the ability of the borrowers' ability to pay it back. Yes, governments can always print money to repay the debt and governments can work together to ignore certain manifest facts, but if people lose faith in the idea of money, no amount of printing will save the global economy. Oh, and be reminded that when I speak of a meager $66 trillion, I'm just talking about what's called "sovereign" or government-issued debt. Further consideration of total debt—including personal loans, mortgages, and corporate debt—takes these figures so far beyond ludicrous that any discussion of actual repayment of all debt, everywhere, morphs into a discussion of the metaphysical. There's not enough physical paper on the planet to print the fiat currency needed to square all the world's debts.

Yes, well-meaning governments issue debt for various good reasons. In theory, they do so to provide the "juice" required to keep a healthy and expanding economy humming. While few would dispute that this is a necessary task, when the amount of juice added to the system exceeds the ability of the economy to use it, and this continues year after year, the economy will become dysfunctional. That is exactly where we are. The global economy is functioning, but it's not healthy and is creating a massive imbalance in the system.

Global governments have and will continue to flood the economic system with debt that won't be paid off without massively disrupting the system. No one government is to blame, and no one government can break the global economy, but when most if not all of our major governments continuously create too much artificial stimulus to keep the party going, we'll all be harmed once the juice no longer works. One way or another, the purchasing power of every citizen with any net worth to speak of will be diminished, and that is the best-case scenario.

I'm no professional economist, and even if I were I wouldn't suggest that anyone bank on the specifics of my forecasts. However, I am an ultra-thinker who has studied and gauged the economy from every conceivable angle. I am a person who has a good understanding of economics. I can tell you it is extremely likely, just short of a certainty, that our country's sovereign debt will not be repaid, ever. If we, the largest and most diverse economy in the world, can't repay our debt there is no way lesser countries, economically speaking, can repay theirs. Mine is not a prediction of the specifics but a statement of the obvious.

With my own ignorance of the details admitted, it seems to me that the best predictor of the future is the past. Therefore, as I visualize just how this whole unfortunate dilemma plays out, I suspect governments will continue to do what they've been doing unless or until it no longer works. I don't expect an abrupt reset or devaluation at some given date. Whatever happens will be slow and methodical if at all possible. Governments don't like big abrupt changes. They prefer to sneak up on their citizens as they spout off half-truths and innuendo.

Most of the larger countries are attempting to monetize their debt. In short, this means sovereign debt is paid back by issuing more debt and/or the printing of additional fiat currency. The effect is a dilution of overall value, but the holder of the newly issued debt doesn't notice that values have been diminished as long as others play along. Everyone prefers to play along because currency is interchangeable. I don't want your currency to be worth less, because the implicit value of your dollar is equal to those I myself carry.

One would believe such a transformation of debt to freshly printed currency would lead to price inflation. Inflation, as you know, increases the value of tangible assets, and as it does, a buyer's purchasing power is diminished. It's measured in percentages. To say the annual inflation rate is 5% infers something would cost 5% more next year than this year. In theory, we should be experiencing significant inflation here in 2020, but we hardly notice a hint of it. The experts tell us we aren't seeing inflation today mainly because when it comes to a system as large and vibrant as the global economy there are many crosscurrents that offset inflationary pressures. The timing is unpredictable at best, but they say inflation will happen eventually. Still, before that day comes, any number of other things may happen. Believe it or not there are models that indicate before inflation occurs the global economy will go through a period of deflation.

Deflation is the worst possible circumstance for a free market economy. Deflation is represented by declining wages, prices, and asset values. Think of it this way. If the price of an iPhone was $1,200 today and understood to be $1,000 next week and then $900 the following, wouldn't the number of iPhone buyers today shrink? What if your own wages went down by 20% per year for several years in a row? What if the value of your largest single asset, your home, regularly declined in value by a percentage point per month? How much confidence would you have in buying any big-ticket item?

When deflation has occurred in the past, basically everybody loses. Sure, if you could somehow act before anyone else to protect yourself, you could attempt to move assets quickly, putting the majority of your net worth into long-term and zero-coupon bonds. Unfortunately, this strategy assumes there is no inherent currency risk associated with whatever circumstances caused the deflation in the first place. This would probably be a flawed assumption. With that said, assuming the period of deflation was a short-term event investing in long bonds might work to preserve value. Still, even if you knew what to do, the reality is you'd likely find that you'd acted way too late. The bond prices were bid up in the blink of an eye, so you still paid too much. The only likely winners in a period of deflation will be the wealthiest of insiders who with the questionable assistance of others managed to "predict" deflation before the rest of us had even seen the print.

During a period of deflation, the rare group of winners tend to be those who don't participate in the economy anyway. Global economic models are built upon an assumption of inflation not deflation; therefore, efforts are continually made to manage a small level of inflation while stabilizing optimal interest rates. The system itself becomes challenged when faced with deflation because the formulas assume a positive cost of capital. When capital costs remain at, near, or below zero the formula informs us that we should sit on the sidelines and not participate in the system. What's the system? It's the global economy. During a deflationary period, it makes sense to sit on the sidelines and not engage in commerce. The problem is we can't all sit out; otherwise, we'd have no economy left and all go broke.

In their efforts to keep their economies functioning, interest rates from rising too fast, and encourage inflation, governments have made massive amounts of "cheap money" available. Cheap money is money loaned at ridiculously low interest rates. This has created an interest rate-driven building boom, production surpluses, and historically high investment asset prices. Bad investment decisions are masked by lending money out at extremely low interest rates. It is no secret that every major city on the globe is experiencing a building boom. Why? Cheap money lowers the cost of capital and encourages the construction of new projects that under normal circumstances wouldn't be built. When capital itself is on sale and this continues for years, what we're left with is a number of less than ideal office complexes, factories, ports, warehouses, apartments, and homes.

Further proof of our messed-up system is evident through a measure referred to as the velocity or turnover of money. Every dollar turns over, and this turnover rate acts as a multiplier enhancing the impact of dollars within the system. Money velocity is a calculation of the speed of movement of dollars within the economy. In theory, it will accelerate when the economy is humming and decelerate when the system is anticipating a downturn. In our current situation, the economy appears relatively strong, but the velocity of money continues to slow. The conflicting signal appears to indicate that the system is failing to absorb all of the dollars efficiently. As a result, the impact of any given dollar is not as meaningful as it has been in the past.

Governments across the planet are taking advantage of the too much money dynamic by issuing investment products (bonds) for the surplus money to buy. Unfortunately for them and us, they're compounding what will already be a very big problem. An incredible amount of new debt has been issued in the past five to ten years. This is far more debt than is necessary to fund their needs, but because there are willing buyers of debt, they can't resist filling the demand. Debt eventually needs to be repaid, and at some point, it will become obvious that sovereign nations have no real way or even a plan to pay off their debts. The global economy is barely absorbing the surplus now and will fail at some point in the future.

When will that happen? It's already starting to happen in certain parts of the globe. As this failure to manage the money surplus spreads, market values will reset or reprice. Governments will attempt to game the system as long as they can until it becomes obvious that citizens across the globe have lost faith in the global economy. Whether this event results in inflation, deflation, debt monetization, or outright formal devaluation is unimportant. What is critically important is that for many this will be the third investment disaster of the past thirty years, and it will last longer than either of the others. Many people simply won't have enough time to recover from this major financial event.

My supposition is those who overweight what proves to be the worst-performing asset categories will be virtually wiped out during this period, while those who maintain pure diversification will experience losses but not so grave as to be destroyed. From my ultra-thinking which is based on fair-minded considerations, I believe that the disruptions to come will reduce one's net worth by between 20% and 70%. My figures aren't intended to be precise. They are simply based on my ultra-thinking. No person or machine can predict a complex dynamic system like our global economy. Still, we can make educated guesses and act with forethought to defend ourselves from the likely. Something will happen. I put my money on a bet that it will happen within the next ten years. If I'm wrong, fine. I won't live more than thirty more years anyway, so what have I lost? Some opportunities for a bit of added wealth? What do I gain if I'm correct? Probably nothing, but I likely saved 20% to 70% of my existing net worth.

This major financial slowdown—long-term recession, depression, financial reset, or whatever phrase you like to use—will happen. I'm convinced of the result. I've created this belief within my own delusion and must live within my reality. People in their fifties and sixties had better heed my warning. What I'm telling you is that a person's accumulation of value in all of their financial assets will be discounted by a significant amount within ten years. There will probably be no place of absolute refuge, and if there is we won't recognize it as such until most of the trouble has passed. Some investment assets will hold up better than others. Which will do better and by how much? I have my guesses, but I don't personally rely on my own guess, so I'm sure not going to apprise my readers of them.

Anyone's expert guess of the eventual winners and losers shouldn't be banked on, in my opinion, which is why I recommend absolute diversification. Still, I do have some more specific ideas in regard to how things might play out in our country. Let's start by doing a better job of defining what I mean by a phrase like "troubling economic times." Troubling is probably an understatement. Think U.S. financial depression worse than those you've read of during the 1930s. Times will be worse than any of us have ever seen, but I don't believe our fellow citizens will let others starve if they can help it. Think of possibly being unemployed or significantly underemployed for twenty years. You'd easily qualify for government aid under such circumstances; however, the government might be proven to have less than you.

With regards to real estate ... home, condo, and apartment rents will go up dramatically for several reasons. The first is that the majority of rentals built in the last decade have been those in the high-end price range. Second, property tax and insurance costs will undoubtedly increase, and those increases will need to be passed on to tenants. Finally, interest rate rises will increase the carrying costs of investment real estate. In contrast to this overall trend, single-family home rents will decline in the suburbs. Unfortunately, people won't want to live in the suburbs.

Real estate values, in general, will be depressed, and the worst segments will be higher-end suburban homes and commercial office space. There will be a massive surge in suburban sellers as folks seek to cash-in before the "worst." But it all happens too quickly. A surplus of abandoned homes will be the end result within three to four years after the collapse in suburban home values. This breaks the residential real estate market and further compounds government debt issues because it is the federal government that has insured home loans which will soon be in default. The real estate market stays broken for well over a decade—maybe thirty or even fifty years!

The healthcare system is broken now, and things will get far worse in the near future. True, the actual product of care may get better, but the execution of delivery and payment for said care will get worse. The U.S. Congress has failed. They've neglected to pass any reform, and now the healthcare system has fallen below the point of rescue. The health insurance premium model and so-called formulary model for pricing we've used for roughly fifty years will need to be completely scrapped. Let me put it plainly: *healthcare will be rationed.* What this means is if you are old, frail, infirm, morbidly obese, or simply don't have a healthcare advocate who can step in and speak on your behalf, you'll be in trouble very soon. I urge you to get in better health, get a physical, get in shape while you can because within twenty-four to thirty-six months of the collapse of our healthcare model all bets are off.

It is no secret that both England and Canada ration healthcare. The way their system works, if say, you're fifty-five years old, are overweight, and smoke, sure you can get in line for that "free" heart surgery, but you'll be so far back in the line you'll die well before your number is called. If you've got stage IV cancer and need help, your number of priority is not higher than one with stage III. It's lower simply because your odds of full recovery are lower. Furthermore, if you're eighty-five years old and in great health, forget about getting knee surgery. The government has mathematically determined that your knees are a waste of money for the simple "fact" that you'll be dead in five years anyway. Only the best prospects move to the front of the line. Care isn't rationed on a first-come, first-served basis but through the use of a cost-benefit analytic.

I suggest you form your own view of what it will mean to you personally when and if the world moves into a prolonged period of economic distress rather than rely on my own delusion. Each person will face their own challenges. Once you ultra-think what yours are likely to be, you can better prepare. Just remember you'll be somewhat wrong, but that doesn't matter. You're better off by planning than not, and there's virtually no downside to preparation.

CHAPTER 13

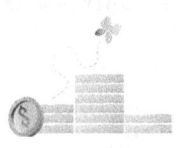

# PREDICTIONS OF A MIND MEANT TO INSPIRE ANOTHER

My tendency, my mental inclination, is to plan for the worst and hope for the best. Your own may be quite different. You may see the world as moving toward bliss. Therefore, when you plan for an economic disaster, perhaps after ultra-thinking you believe the government can and will act in ways to make life even better than before, that's fine with me. I hope you're right and that I'm proven rather foolish for taking the steps I do.

Still, I must plan as I do because I am who I am. I can't shut down my mind and don't believe I should even try. So while my own predictions, a delusion of my own creation, might seem to portent a rather bleak future they are actually neutral. I don't fear the future because I know I can't really control it anyway. All I can control is within my own head; therefore, I must embrace the flawed individual I am while continually attempting to improve this being. Humans are blessed to think, and I urge more thoughts not less. We won't be creatures who act like dogs, wonderful creatures in their own right, simply reacting to every stimulus which comes our way.

What I do deeply fear is getting rolled by an event that in my gut just seemed like it was going to happen. My personal action bothers no one, so I'm at liberty to do as I choose. Please don't assume I'm a negative person. Far from it, I'm actually quite optimistic. So optimistic that I'd attempt to write a book in the expectation that you'll be urged to pause and reconsider your own money myths. Still, I'll never let my optimistic hope override prudence. Why? Because I've determined that the only thing important to me personally is reconciling my self-created reality to the best version of myself that I can live with.

I do understand the irony of my own listing of predictions in the face of my recurring proclamation that specific economic events can't be predicted accurately. The point I'm attempting to make is that while accurate predictions remain elusive, one should attempt to make the best and most fair-minded of predictions for the simple fact that we are thinking creatures. Your mind is nothing but a forecasting machine. You are predicting even though you're unaware. By contemplating my specific predictions, you'll gain insight into your own. Once you are aware of your predictions and assumptions about the future, an ideological perspective may become more apparent. You can then start to reconsider your own wisdom. Is your assessment of the future a well-informed and fair-minded view, or simply a reflexive view based upon historical narrative?

With my explanation documented, let's take a look at a few rather specific but somewhat random personal predictions.

**Lifestyle and Social Trends**
- Expatriation explodes in popularity as tens of thousands of citizens seriously consider and a few even manage to leave the U.S. The government responds by enforcing tax policies that seek to capture wealth and income at the source. Watch for both federal and state laws that don't allow for the remittance of pension and social security payments without a mandatory tax withholding of 20% or more.

- Expats, as you know, aren't technically expatriated; however, their numbers also explode from a few million to many tens of millions of people.

- Pets become more desirable than children in many communities. More pet parks, pet sitters, and pet trainers are needed. Watch for branded pet leashes, tags, and collars which become desired accessories touting pet celebrities of both the human and beast variety.
- Riverboats, cruising barges, and houseboats become more and more popular. Riverfront communities that spot the trend benefit immensely by providing destinations for river travelers. Theme-based river ports entice travelers to stay awhile and take in the local fare. You will even start to see a huge shore excursion business be created. Buses, much like those seen in Europe, will start moving travelers inland to see the local sites. The U.S. Army Corps of Engineers will be challenged to keep up with demand from river cities that seek authorized river improvements.
- The number of students in public schools, as a percentage of the population, drops tremendously within ten years. The cost of private education, homeschooling, or even small group tutoring drops as retiring teachers seek secondary employment. Retired teachers take up gig assignments offering six- to twelve-week sessions which either augment the failing public school system or replace traditional methods of education altogether. Standardized testing urges further growth of the trend as it becomes quite obvious that the child who benefited from the "new" model gets better scores. Public schools become the second if not the last choice selected by informed parents.
- After wide acceptance is first gained, people start to unplug from home-assistance technology. It comes to be seen as simply too much information. People install master switches that allow them to constantly unplug and

re-plug at their whim rather than leaving devices on autopilot. Personal privacy becomes a legislative issue once again. A handful of privacy cases, particularly those impacting children, support the unplug trend.
- The myth of retirement is exposed for what it is: a way to free up employment opportunities for the young. Retirement was an idea that came to be promoted on the heels of the Great Depression. At that time, the U.S. economy was stuck; there were a huge number of unemployable younger people in major metropolitan areas. The U.S. government decided to bring in an "old-age pension" as a means to encourage older workers to step aside. This created job openings for new workers. Given the fact that retirement isn't a mandatory requirement in the vast majority of jobs, people stop retiring en masse. By 2030, more people are working past their "normal" social security retirement age than those who formally retire.
- Google, Microsoft, and Amazon struggle to keep from being broken up by regulators and fail. However, the regulation has limited effect because the U.S. federal government relies on the data just as much as the firms. The odds are 50/50 as to whether breaking up the companies actually does much of anything other than allowing Congress to claim credit for action.
- The Amazon model continues to decimate the business of retail. Big-box retailers survive but cut back on slow-moving merchandise or items which are frequently price shopped by consumers. If the item is something that typically is studied before it is bought, you won't find it in stock at your big-box store. These stores will have large warehouses and offer same-day delivery, but the physical items presented in the store are simply demos.

- The popularity of auto ownership, homeownership, and "stuff" in general will continue to decline. Owning stuff, and even selecting stuff, is soon considered a waste of time, effort, and money. We have too much information. The paradox of choice becomes a real problem for many. In revolt, buyers simply step out to hang out rather than choosing to check out. Consumers of the future will spend far less than their predecessors. Money, celebrity, and flamboyance, in general, fall out of favor, as do superstar athletic contracts.
- Spending significant time in coffee shops, bars, bookstores, and even public parks becomes more popular than pricey vacations. Many simply opt for nothing. Minimalism and frugality become very fashionable.

**Healthcare and Insurance**
- Insurance is a model of risk transference, nothing more. Our modern conception of this model has become misunderstood particularly as it relates to medical insurance. We pay a premium and have come to assume this premium entitles us to transfer our obligation to pay to an insurance company in all circumstances. Therefore, we've changed the definition of the idea of risk transference to payment transference. As a result, the business of health insurance will be mostly out of business within ten years.
- Private healthcare moves rapidly toward a clinic model, replacing the general practice model wherein you simply pay a deductible for medical care as advised by one professional.
- Concierge medical, the model wherein customers pay a membership fee in addition to the cost of medical care, becomes the only realistic option apart from the clinic

model. A very limited number of physicians move from clinics to concierge, provided their customers deem their service worth the three- to ten-thousand-dollar annual fee charged simply to be part of a particular physician's clientele.
- The formulary prescription drug pricing model finally falls. That model sets prescription prices based on whatever the local insurance market will bear. Such formulary pricing is deemed evil by the consumer as it starts to become obvious that the model allows sellers and insurance companies to reap superior profits. Congress takes up the issue in a bipartisan manner, and by 2030, drug prices are more or less the same across the U.S. regardless of payer or insurance company.
- Private health insurance technically remains available, but like concierge medical care, it is extremely pricey. The federal government will soon offer a guaranteed issue healthcare policy which is significantly different than that of private insurance.

**Real Estate**
- Housing prices continue to rise and fall, but the overall trend will be down, not up as it has been the past fifty or more years.
- The real estate market becomes even more bifurcated. There will be a few distinct groups of huge winners and a massive hoard of big losers. The old adage that "all real estate is local" will be truer in the future than it is today.
- The price of so-called mini mansion homes in the suburbs will decline rather consistently for years, while affordable homes within ten miles of major urban areas will hold up much better in the collapse.

- Driven by cash sales, the ultra-high-end home and condo market does surprisingly well as the rich seek safe-haven investments. The uber-wealthy seem to protect themselves and this micro-market of investment real estate.
- A Silver Tsunami of move-up homes floods the real estate market as boomers scramble to unload these homes which, in theory, hold the majority of their net worth. This happens sometime before 2030. The vast majority of sellers in this relatively brief cycle never realize the paper gains they so hoped to convert to dollars. They become house poor as they continue to pay taxes, insurance, and maintenance costs on homes they simply can't sell for a "fair" price.
- Eventually, significant numbers of seniors simply give up on selling altogether. Walking away from their home, which still has a mortgage, means they knowingly ruin their credit rating. However, they've come to appreciate that such a measure of creditworthiness is meaningless when they don't plan on making any major purchases anyway.
- What had once been the preferred move-up subdivisions become the new depressed neighborhoods.
- Investors struggle to find good tenants when the properties themselves continually sell at huge discounts. Suburban rents fall and stay low for an extended period. It will cost no more to rent a mini mansion than an efficiency apartment downtown.
- Commercial office space prices collapse in a manner never seen before. Co-work space poses a very serious challenge to traditional office space, but the problem is more systemic and can't be blamed on the co-work space trend. Entire buildings will be left vacant for years forcing cities

to come up with creative solutions to stem urban blight. If you believe it was bad when a couple of blocks of residential houses fell into disarray, wait until you see downtown areas the size of the financial district of Manhattan vacated. There will be hundreds of vacant high-rises offering millions of rentable square feet which no company on the globe actually needs. This will happen within a decade. I'm quite confident in this prediction.

- Coastal living trends have peaked, and more people will start to reconsider their choice to live in hurricane-prone areas. National flood insurance simply becomes unaffordable. As a result, only the most elite properties remain viable. It simply doesn't make sense to insure a $400,000 beach bungalow when the insurance and real estate taxes costs $50,000 a year. Lower-end properties will be replaced, and the number of people actually living in coastal areas will decline. The average citizen can't afford to take the risk of going without insurance. Their more modest properties will be converted into high-end vacation rentals owned by investment pools who can self-insure.
- Casual short-term rentals come under more scrutiny and will be largely regulated out of business in many local markets. The Airbnb trend has peaked and will become exceedingly regulated simply because it pushes rents higher, compounding the problems associated with maintaining affordable housing. Smart regulators are slow to react but will, within the next few years, start to aggressively enforce regulations that will require leases of three months or more.

## Raw Economics

- The $100 U.S. bill will be phased out quietly within a decade. The official reason is fraud and the exportation of greenbacks abroad. The real reason is that the Federal Reserve is moving the public toward acceptance of digital currency and needs to make it more difficult for citizens to remain off the grid of U.S. money control.
- The reserve status of the U.S. dollar and the global SWIFT banking system are in doubt. Reserve status allows the U.S. to remain the standard measure for the vast majority of global transactions. Technology will change this dynamic as financial systems come to offer real-time currency conversion against some sort of global currency basket. The new basket won't be the reserve currency officially; however, it will negate the need for foreign governments to hold USDs. The implication is that billions of dollars will be freed up within the global economic system influencing a weaker dollar trend.
- In the near term, the U.S. dollar will remain relatively strong against global competition until reserve status is hopelessly lost.
- Retail banking comes to take on a concierge-type model where customers pay for the privilege of using a bank. Banking then becomes a luxury service, and the average consumer is forced into an online banking model.
- Cryptocurrency or cyber-currency, like Bitcoin, is allowed to flourish, and its value may reach unprecedented heights. Still, regulators are devising ways to usurp the features of crypto through competing platforms. Some suggest crypto and its cousin blockchain technology will defy any attempts to stymie its proliferation. I somewhat agree; however, I do recognize that the Federal Reserve

Bank and U.S. taxing authorities have put a number of alternative currencies out of business over the past several decades. It is possible that once the federal government moves citizens toward acceptance of digital currency the government then puts forth legislation that significantly hinders the use of any digital currency other than that which is officially authorized.

- The heyday of publicly-traded stock and bond markets is coming to a close, and things will get really ugly! The next big market correction will highlight the fundamental flaw of market-weighted exchange-traded funds and hedging strategies. The flaw is that most investors are using the same instruments and underlying strategies to protect themselves from a market downturn. These strategies are valid, but only if the strategy is followed by a relatively small number of investors. This should be obvious, but evidently, it isn't. When we have a big correction, huge numbers of investors will attempt to activate their protection strategy. It won't work! Investors will find the exit clogged with other like-minded astute investors. There is absolutely no way, in my own humble opinion, that any of the commonly promoted protection strategies will work en masse.

- The publicly traded markets will cease to be functioning markets at the height of the next major downturn. If we're fortunate, markets will reopen daily and allow an orderly sell-off lasting weeks, months, or even years. If we're unlucky, the market will be raided by investors holding metaphorical pitchforks and demanding that their investments be sold at any price. Either result won't be good. Market confidence will collapse and won't recover for at least twenty or thirty years.

- Private investment markets will become the choice of smarter investors, and that trend has already begun. It is becoming an open secret on Wall Street that the real money is made before a security goes public. Of course, private markets are closed to the average investor, so "smart" money is left to the pickings of multimillionaires. The general public, via their 401(k) accounts, ends up having to choose between dumb and dumber investments, most of which are exchange-traded index funds which will soon be decimated as previously discussed.
- The U.S. government may come to issue new debt at negative interest rates. With that said, it is entirely possible that "official rates" remain positive while "real rates" (those obtained when a bond is actually sold) become negative. Regardless of whether they are official or real interest rates, all bets will be off if the global economic system is forced to digest such rates for more than a couple of years. Technically, capitalism as an economic model doesn't work if the cost of capital goes below zero. Financial models themselves only work with positive numbers. Negative interest rates simply don't calculate!

I could go on, but I'm less confident in several other predictions than those presented here. Whether you agree with many or none of my predictions, I hope you take a moment to think about where our economy is headed. Once you do, I'm confident that you'll be better prepared to make personal financial decisions that harmonize with your worldview. For instance, if you believe home values are very likely to reach new highs, and you sell today simply because a neighbor's home sold for top dollar, you'll be kicking yourself for selling if your belief is proven correct. On the other hand, if you have confidence that housing prices have topped out and you don't sell when you can, you'll be upset that you didn't. You need to take actions that make sense to you. If you're true to yourself, you'll be better able to sit with the result either way. Happiness is a mind thing, nothing more.

I take for granted that you have more than a passing interest in personal finance; otherwise, you'd be doing something else this very moment. People tend to do what they want. As a person who takes their finances seriously, I suspect you may be familiar with some of the so-called "tried and true" secrets to financial success. You've heard them: buy-and-hold, invest in your 401(k) or IRA, pay yourself first, live on a budget, etc. Don't get me wrong, these may be great ideas, but—and I do speak from experience—if the motto doesn't fit with the way you think, such a theme simply won't work. A dog will hunt, and a squirrel will gather. A dog forced to sit on a stack of bones is one rather unhappy dog.

People need to take some time to get to know themselves, recognizing their own tendencies, both good and bad. These tendencies present a manifestation of the ways you deal with money. Once understood, you will gain insight into your own money myths. An appreciation that these are nothing but ideas within a mind will allow you to put them on the shelf, at least temporarily, in order to re-consider their worthiness from a perspective that is fair-minded. Your existing ideas may prove themselves to be ideal, or not. That is entirely your call.

You've proven that you're open to the idea that the mind drives happiness by reading this book. We probably agree that ideas, I call them myths, about money influence feelings of happiness one way or another. We've explored my own myths, my money delusions, many of which have been reduced to predictions about the economy. I urge you now to attempt to make your own predictions because it will help you match your financial goals to your deep-seated feelings about money.

To prime your mind to contemplate your own money myths, consider the following questions.

1. How seriously do you take predictions that major economic challenges are very likely to occur within the coming decade?
2. How long will you and/or your life partner be alive?
3. How much net worth do you have, how's it spread (allocated), and is it even worth protecting?
4. Finally, is it in your nature to act, or are you basically a person who simply procrastinates so much that even if you wanted to act you probably wouldn't anyway?

Okay, that last question had a rather harsh tone. However, I'm being harsh to stress my larger point, and it is not that you must plan. Yes, I think you should seriously consider your own finances, but if you are historically one who prefers to sit on the sidelines don't beat yourself up for being who you are. I *think* you should plan, but you don't *have* to plan. Keep that statement in mind.

Your life is your own. Sure, it's possible that another's poor financial decisions or lack of planning for a rather foreseeable event will impact you or I. But, while their acts probably weren't ideal, I doubt they were immoral or evil. You are the person you create, and it's not my right to dictate to you. When we encounter people who, in our own opinion, are not acting responsibly with regards to their finances, or life for that matter, we need to let it go. Yes, we can try to influence them out of love for the individual, concern for our shared humanity, or even a vain quest to sell a few books. Still, in the end, does it really matter to me what you do? In my view, and this too may sound harsh, as long as you don't camp on my lawn, steal my stuff, or infringe on my own tranquility go ahead and do whatever you like. Just pause and occasionally think about your choices from a fair-minded perspective.

CHAPTER 14

# A TIME TO PROTECT AND THE WORTHMIX MODEL

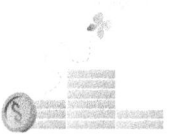

As a person who overemphasizes reason and logic, very much a left-brain oriented person, I step back and view my own ideas on the proverbial shelf. It seems I tend to predict the worst. I like to think of myself as a pragmatist, but since you don't know me, you probably read me as a pessimist. I want to assume things will work out, but I also want to assume I will win at the dollar slots in Las Vegas. Given I don't have the emotional energy to withstand another dot-com crash, housing bubble pop, or 2008–2009 financial meltdown, and I believe similar events will occur within the decade I must plan ahead. Obviously, I don't want to be negative. My leaning toward logic dominates my mind—sometimes for the best, sometimes not. It is what it is.

As a financial professional, I've worked with thousands of people over the past thirty years, and without a doubt, there is one absolute way to obtain financial peace of mind: reconcile yourself to keenly understood personal beliefs and principles. It's not about better investment performance. Performance ebbs and flows. Success in accumulation of value is sometimes the result of personal decisions; other times, dumb luck is the decider. Understanding why and how you've obtained the net worth you have today is an exercise in futility. There are simply too many things that could've dropped one way or another. You can play the odds, but in the end, it is as it is.

On the other hand, the self can be rather understood. Ultra-thinking life, ideas, and ideas about money can help you gain that understanding. I've spent decades attempting to understand myself and know I'm closer today than I was before I started this book. Still, the journey will continue simply because the self changes incessantly given the mind's contemplation. Despite the fluidity of mind, I consistently feel an impulse to plan and protect. To do either, I must predict despite the fact I may be wasting a great deal of effort. I actively seek out alternative ideas, contemplate with what I believe is a fair mind, and update my own conclusions as a result.

These predictions are my Ultrathoughts about what I deem plausible for us in the United States in the coming decade. From my personal experience, I believe it's safe for me to assume I'll be correct with 20–30% of these predictions. If I'm very lucky, I'll approach a 50% accuracy rate. Regardless, I'll bet on myself. That way I'll have personal peace of mind.

In my myth, I assume big changes—systemic changes affecting entire markets and economies—are very likely to occur in the near future. I offer you absolutely no empirical evidence of my own ideas, my money myths. If you need that sort of thing, buy a book by any number of financial "experts" who use fear to sell books and newsletters. I'm not into scaring people, just helping them clear their head. All I suggest is that you consider the possibility that systemic changes are more likely to happen in the coming decade than not. If massive economic distress does occur and you're wholly unprepared despite your own inclination to get prepared, you're going to be really upset. Furthermore, from a practical standpoint, you may not have enough time on this planet to recover financially. Finally, remember, I'm not talking end-of-the-world *Mad Max* stuff here. Significant? Yes. Life ending? No, these changes won't kill you.

It's better for a person's mental health to succeed or fail based on their own decisions rather than those of others. When you bet on yourself you are more likely to maintain a positive attitude. To bet on yourself wisely, you should first make sure the supposition at hand is not a reflexive view fed to you by society but a deeply felt truth. All you can do is your best. You win emotionally simply by doing the best you can to make quality decisions based on Ultrathoughts derived from your fair mind.

Protection of your net worth in times of financial distress is best accomplished by focusing on four very general objectives:

1. Stay nimble. Make sure you do all you can to maintain adequate, readily available financial resources to live on for at least one or two years. The old rule of thumb was a safety net of three to six months of cash in the bank. My new rule is one or two years' worth and some of that money should be cash in hand. I'll leave discussions about food, shelter, and defense to other folks, but suffice to say, get prepared on every conceivable level.

2. Get and stay as healthy as you can: mentally, spiritually, and physically. Your friends, family, and certainly your partner doesn't need the obligation of taking care of you. Take a walk, join a club, join a synagogue, train for a run, beat in a drum circle, write a book, sing a song, whatever; get your act together. Live your life with confidence and a smile on your face.

3. Make every effort to minimize unsecured debt. If you simply won't do this, you may want to position yourself for an expeditious and legal bankruptcy proceeding. For that, consult an attorney. Don't take legal advice from a friend, accountant, or Google. There is good debt and bad debt. Pay off the bad debt. And, for goodness sake,

don't waste time by consolidating debt without first adjusting your lifestyle. It won't work!
4. Diversify, diversify, diversify your investable net worth.
   A. Seek bank diversification using multiple FDIC insured banks.
   B. Seek location and marketplace diversification for investment real estate, stocks, bonds, and even safe storage. Never be bound to one region, market, or location if at all possible.
   C. Maintain investment asset category diversification using some type of model which makes sense to you. I suggest no less than five broad classifications.

In this section, I'd like to take a few pages to discuss investment asset allocation using my own personal model I call the WorthMix. With that said, mine is simply an example based upon my own impressions about the future and not a specific investment recommendation.

The WorthMix model is all about the protection of net worth because I assume that attempts at offense are a waste of effort. Offense takes chances, sometimes makes aggressive bets, and lives with the results. My model makes one bet: don't bet on offense. I spread investment risk to such an extent that any big win or loss in any category is muted. As of this writing, I believe I'll stick with the model for a decade and maybe even the rest of my life, but certainly, that could change based on my assumptions about the future. If and when my mind changes, I will not hesitate to change my asset allocation. I don't want to be on defense for the rest of my life, but given my age, maybe I will. In short, I wouldn't have written this chapter had I not honestly believed I will stick with my WorthMix model for at least a decade.

To follow the recommendations of the WorthMix model, I suggest that investable net worth is best allocated or divided between five investment asset categories. The model demands that a specific percentage be allocated into each of the five categories at a fixed percentage. The target or goal is always 20%, give or take 3% in each category. Successful application of the model implies a review and reallocation, also known as rebalancing, every three to nine months.

The categories may sound familiar, but there is some nuance to the descriptions. They are:

1. FDIC CASH: U.S. chartered bank accounts, certificates of deposit, and FDIC insured money market accounts.

2. STREAMS: Bonds, bond mutual funds, money market funds, annuities, pensions, and social security.

3. STOCKS: U.S. based multinational corporate stocks, proven international firm stocks, and equity-oriented mutual funds.

4. INVESTMENT REAL ESTATE: Real estate as an investment and real estate trusts.

5. HARD ASSETS: Gold, silver, tradeables, collectibles, foreign currency, and a supply of U.S. currency.

Obviously, before you can categorize an investment asset you need to fully understand the category. Each has a specific number which implies what I would characterize as an intensity level. Think of the number as representing the strength of a hurricane. For instance, FDIC cash as an investment is pretty plain and dull, so it's a Cat 1. Streams of cash flow like annuities, bonds, and social security are nearly as dull as FDIC cash, but for technical reasons, they aren't. Stocks, as long as they're sellable, are pretty ordinary, so I say they're a Cat 3. Real estate as an investment, Cat 4, starts to get exciting because when the market turns bad you may find it very difficult to sell out of a real estate investment. Still, no classification is more exciting than Cat 5. Cat 5 assets are very risky, often illiquid, and unfortunately can be very stressful to handle. Try storing a collectible for twenty years or selling $100,000 worth of silver coins, and you'll have a new appreciation for my calling an asset category an intensity level 5 investment.

If you wish to use the model and assess your own weighting, remember that when assigning a category, consistency of definition is the key. I thoroughly describe each category in Appendix 2 of the book and attempt to provide you with some insight about each specific category. In the world of accounting, consistency often trumps accuracy. You need to thoroughly understand the categories and be able to say "X investible asset is a Category 1," and "Z asset is a Category 5." Once you make that assessment, try hard to stick with it; henceforth, every time you assess your own situation, you will remain consistent in your own classifications.

With an understanding of the categories, you can assign each asset you have to one of the five. When in doubt, look at the appendix and pick the one category which makes the most sense. Then you'll simply add up the investment asset values per category. Obviously, the total of all five categories will equal your grand total of all investment assets; if not, proof your work and correct the oversight. Remember, there are only five categories. Each and every investment asset (net of any loan value) must be assigned a category. This is your current asset allocation.

It may be helpful to create a pie chart showing the percentage allocated to each category. Take note: are the slices fairly uniform? If so, you're in good shape. If not, get ready to make some decisions. To apply a model like this, you'll probably need to sell some assets, buying underweighted categories in their stead. This process is known as rebalancing your investment portfolio. It is a very important step, and if your allocations are way out of kilter don't rush to rebalance. I suggest you do this over no less than one year, assuming your current weighted percentages are way off their targets. The objective is to equalize the percentages over a relatively short period (one to three years) without being so anxious as to risk selling at the absolute wrong time. With that said, you'll never know what the best price is, and if you procrastinate you won't accomplish the goal. Rebalancing must occur from time to time, otherwise what's the point of having a model?

WorthMix suggests a very basic allocation of your investments in hopes of creating and helping you maintain peace of mind in what I perceive are troubling economic times. In a sense, it allows you to step away from the decision-making process. Once you rely on a strait five category, equally-weighted model, there's not much to do other than rebalancing. Even if I'm wrong about our times, a user of the model will likely obtain peace of mind because no asset category is over- or under-weighted. The model takes all investment assets, categorizes them by similarities into five categories, and suggests an equal weighting. I believe this model offers a significant degree of protection for a person's current investable net worth in a manner that doesn't lock a person into a strategy or preclude them from experiencing investment gains.

WorthMix recognizes that while trends and the opinion of experts can provide some valuable insight, they never give us certainty. Therefore, reliance on either is folly in times of true financial turmoil. You will experience the financial loss when it comes, not the expert; consequently, it is you alone who should decide whether the time is right to abandon the expert. Just maybe you should ignore history and protect yourself as best you can from an ill-defined yet probable systemic economic change. This model is the ultimate "buy it all, sell it all" capitulation to the vagaries of global economics and relies on no opinion whether its one of expert or idiot.

In using this model, I'm always invested; however, I'm certainly not playing the odds in my favor. Historically, some investment categories are more likely to provide better returns than others. To invest in that which is deemed more likely to perform well is to be playing the odds. In my model, I accept no investment odds because I defer to my basic assumption that all bets are off. History is rather meaningless in times of systemic change. The odds are, therefore, irrelevant.

As you measure and categorize your investment assets, I suggest that you ignore any heirloom type of asset in this net worth listing. Although they may have substantial value, heirloom assets are irrelevant to the model because you've made a decision not to use them under any circumstance. They are heirlooms—not investments. Farms, family jewelry, Great-granddad's cabin—these are typical heirloom investments.

With that said, if you're like many of us, your personal residence (real estate) may be a mix of heirloom and investment real estate. The assumption is that you'd at some point pass down a home to your heirs. In such a case, a secondary calculation is in order. You'd need to calculate the "surplus equity" in the home and determine what is truly an investment (something you'd be willing to spend or lose) or heirloom (something you'd absolutely never sell or jeopardize). You'd then split the value, reporting only the value truly considered and investment you'd spend for purposes of living without remorse.

In making your investable asset list don't overstress things. For valuation, use an appraisal, statement, estimation, or wild guess. Far too many people get stuck attempting to calculate perfect values and end up calculating no values in their quest for perfection. Over time, you'll get better at estimating, and eventually your numbers will be quite good. Still, if this is entirely new to you, the first couple of times you make your list the process can seem a bit overwhelming. If that is the case, you're probably including way too much detail.

When using a model based on current values, often we're forced to use casual estimates. It's simply not practical to get precise values of something like investment real estate as of one exact date. This informs you that you need some flexibility in assessing when to rebalance or not. In your allocation, if the variance is less than about three percent of your grand total, I wouldn't worry much about it. If you worry too much about a percent or two, you're missing a key point of the model. Yes, the model is designed to protect your investible net worth, but the overarching purpose of the model is peace of mind. I urge you to think of the WorthMix as a casual method to spread your investment assets rather than consider it as a formula for financial success.

Of course, all variations won't be small and insignificant. It is suggested that if you are over or under allocated by more than a few percentage points consistently, then you should take notice and consider action. Sell something and buy something else. Again, consistency is the key: consistent valuation methods, consistent category assignments, and consistently sticking with an asset allocation model which will require regular rebalancing. If you can't or won't be consistent, don't use any asset allocation model.

You need to attempt to estimate all values as of the same date if at all possible. For simplicity, most people use quarter-end statements and values, but any date is fine. If you can't for whatever reason use one specific date for all assets, get as close as you can. Within a week will suffice. Frankly, for most assets, even a month or two won't make much difference as long as the economy is relatively stable overall.

Regarding investment real estate values, remember, if you're off a few thousand dollars one side or another it probably won't be a big issue. It typically costs 5–9% to sell real estate, so you might want to discount even paid-off real estate by some amount. Be reminded that for valuation purposes you should not use something called "Full Cash Value" as provided by your county real estate recorder's office. These values don't mean what they appear to mean. These valuations are specifically used for purposes of tax assessment and often have very little bearing on a property's actual value in the open market. If the market is strong, discount your estimate; if it's soft, discount the estimate more. Whatever you do, with regards to real estate values, don't be optimistic. Real estate is very difficult to sell in times of stress, so be conservative in your valuation.

Finally, remember we're only concerned with larger things of value. A $1,000 item won't matter. Assets worth at least a few thousand dollars which are owned because you believe they either hold value or appreciate in value over time should be what's included. Most people wouldn't include things like autos and household items; however, valuable and marketable collectibles are included. When you're considering whether or not to list something like a paid-off car, even if that car is a $130,000 Porsche, don't include it if it's not owned to make or keep your money. If you're *using* this car, you're using it up, so it's not an investment asset. Once you've listed everything and pegged a net value to each, calculate the grand total of your investable assets.

To consistently use the model and fully buy into the idea that we're seeking protection and peace of mind, you need to attempt to ignore investment performance. Yes, over the past eighty or ninety years publicly traded stocks have done quite well, and many advisors shout the benefits of owning. Real estate agents often tell us real estate is the ultimate investment in the long run, so they tend to promote the belief that you can't go wrong with real estate. It is entirely possible that one or more asset categories absolutely explode in value on occasion. Don't take the bait! Stick to the model. Sell out of winners and buy the losers, keeping your focus on having more or less twenty percent of your net investible net worth in each category. Which category of investment asset will be the best performing in the coming decade? Who cares? Pick your expert and email them; it probably won't matter what they say anyway when the economy undergoes systemic change.

Mine is not a proven strategy for superior investment returns. Recall the lottery slogan, "You can't win if you don't play." I cede the point. I won't win by using my model because I'm not actually playing the game of investing. However, I shouldn't lose big either. For the most part, financial experts suggest that we overweight some investments more than others. In the past, I've said those exact words. But times are different in my view. Most of the experts are not considering the increased likelihood of a systemic change. Think big change.

Think the outrageous: no mortgage loans, no U.S. dollar reserve currency, a new global taxing authority, a new global crypto dollar. The global economic system is in danger, and when it falters all bets are off. There may be no winners, just a varying degree of losers.

As you ultra-think your own finances and come to form an idea of your own financial future, you must assess your tolerance for investment loss. Ask yourself what would happen if you lost 25% of your investment value in a couple of days? What if you lose 50% of the value of all of your investments—your home, your 401(k) balance, all of it—and that loss sticks for the next two or three years? What will you do at the end of year three? Now, consider that loss lasting a decade, two, or three? Visualize your net worth today, and assume that it is cut by half, two-thirds, three-quarters! What then?

Seek investment advice from a professional who fully understands you if you want information about past performance and risk of loss. Maybe you'd be well served by that advice; however, I'm telling you that we're going to see some challenges, and you need to appreciate that it is you alone who takes the financial hit. Selecting the supposed optimal category is folly in times of systemic change.

If you would have asked me to provide you with advice a decade or two ago, I'd have likely said more or less what your financial advisor will tell you. I certainly would have given you my opinion and urged you to listen to me. No more specific investment advice will be given. I buy all of them, I sell all of them, and today I focus on the allocation targets. Though my instinct and training inform me that I am buying at least two if not three inferior categories of assets, I have sequestered my logical left-leaning mind. I have, in effect, vetoed my own

# Money On A Mind

investment advice and thrown in the towel, spreading my bets and overweighting no asset category.

If you're worried and either don't have the time or the aptitude to get informed about your own finances, seek advice, but take specific investment recommendations with a grain of salt. Read, study, and listen to others, then simply relax for a few days or weeks. Recognize you're only human and can only do what you can. The idea of money is not what defines you, and certainly, you are far more than your finances. You have far more attributes than the value of your investible assets and earnings potential.

Now do something different; refocus on the dilemma and ultra-think. Attempt to free your mind of inclination and seriously contemplate the challenge of maintaining, or even potentially building, your financial portfolio in a precarious economic environment. Only then will you make a decision which provides peace of mind: an Ultrathought about personal finance.

Your own Ultrathoughts regarding asset allocation may very well include picking a category and investing all your money there. It may also be to subscribe to a theory of your favorite financial guru. That's fine; you've given it some ultra-thinking. Do what you want. Your goal is peace of mind grounded in fair-minded ultra-thinking.

The WorthMix model was conceived after determining that I couldn't adequately gauge the "fair market value" of any investment asset but appreciating that I can't afford to simply sit on the sidelines. Besides … a historically defensive asset category, say hard assets or FDIC cash, might prove to be the most overvalued of all. I ultra-think the environment is nearing a period of great change and probably tremendous challenge. That's my own money myth. Those changes could hurt the accepted values of my investment assets. Still, I need to participate.

I fear there are many bubbles of inflated valuation, but I have no idea how long the bubbles will continue to inflate. As you may know, bubbles are sometimes easy to recognize. The challenge is that most money is made by participating in bubbles. Unfortunately, absolutely nothing but pure luck can predict when or how a bubble bursts.

I was left with a conundrum. How do I participate in multiple bubbles, which I'm pretty sure are bubbles, in a manner which isn't so reckless as to expose myself to financial ruin? Even if I could recognize a bubble, I can't ever understand how to successfully time entry and exit. That's when the Ultrathought hit me: I need a model of absolute diversification, a capitulation that fair value of any investment is questionable at best. Rather than sitting out the bubble period, I'll participate in each and every bubble equally!

I decided on five categories for simplification. The theory was based on my assumption that two bubbles bursting at the same time is very likely. In the worst case, maybe even three or four of my categories would collapse. However, when two or more categories burst, frequently at least one surviving asset class does quite well.

The world is awash in money. The way I view things, when a valuation collapses, any new or remaining money floods into those assets which appear to have weathered the storm. Money always finds a home. A healthy surviving asset class will tend to pick up the surplus, elevating its value in the process. If that one surviving asset class doubles, triples, or even quadruples, my total net worth would not fair too badly.

Of course, if three or four of my five categories fall in value precipitously, it's entirely possible that the entire economy melts down and ceases to function as a system. Banks, insurance companies, and even entire governments could fall. From a balance sheet standpoint, the globe's already underwater. All of the outstanding debt on the planet is well in excess of $250 trillion, and the entire productivity of the world per year is less than one-quarter of that amount—$62 trillion. The bottom line is that little of the sovereignly issued debt on the books today will be permanently repaid. Any macroeconomist or financial scholar understands this. Yet all of this means absolutely nothing, until one day it does.

When the economic system itself fails, millions of people will get hurt financially. A huge percentage of those people will be U.S. citizens who have a significant, say $250,000 to $2.5 million in net worth. These are the folks who will be brought to tears in the collapse if they are unprepared. They probably won't recover financially for the simple fact they won't live long enough. Application of the WorthMix model should, in theory, give those of us in that economic class a better chance of a reasonable recovery. I stop short of recommending it to anyone I don't know, but I do urge you to consider the underlying premise of the model: All financial bets are off in times of systemic economic change.

# CONCLUSION: HAPPINESS

So there you have it—a left-brain oriented CPA has shared what's in his mind. You've heard the rants about a coming financial calamity and of money myths in general. You now have a raw understanding of how ideas of philosophy underpin money and economic theory. That said, you're probably still left with your specific questions about money unanswered. If so, I've accomplished my goal.

I don't want to answer your questions. I want to urge you to find your own answers from a fair mind that has suppressed its innate or historical perspective. When you do that, you'll be ultra-thinking money. Ultra-thinking done well will do more than answer your own questions today. Ultra-thinking will answer these questions for a lifetime and put any money drama you have in its place. It's all a delusion anyway. So don't take it so seriously, and certainly don't let money make you unhappy.

The road to personal happiness for most in our society today probably includes a rest stop called "financial success." The determination of both happiness and success is left to the mind's contemplation influenced by the impression of others. You're happy and you've succeeded financially only when you are content with your circumstance. In the case of your finances, this impression of contentment ultimately has nothing to do with a specific number in your bank account or amount of equity in your home—unless, of course, you so believe. A thousand dollars in the bank will satisfy some, and a million still isn't enough for others.

Studies inform us that our quality of life is significantly influenced by our personal finances. When the very idea of money has a negative influence on your happiness for an extended period of time, stop and adjust something in your life. Whether that means you need to make more money to support your lifestyle, you should spend less time at work, or had better donate to a cause is unimportant. The key point is that when you are unhappy and you determine your money drama is a significant cause of this emotion, it's time to stop. Make a decision. Is this drama worth the price of happiness? If so, fine. Keep doing as you do. If not, I suggest you start by understanding yourself in hopes of learning what is truly important to you.

In order to actually understand yourself, you must delve deep within. When you do, you'll notice how you're thinking and be able to take action accordingly. Since that happiness is purely a mental construct, it seems one would have a difficult time truly creating it without a bit of self-reflection. Yes, a person can be happy without an understanding of self, but creating happiness in the face of a world of distraction and stress is another matter entirely. You can't buy it, nor can you ever be sure you'll keep it.

People can certainly train themselves to adopt a different attitude in an attempt to be happier. Still, unless they devote time to creating different habits of thought, that time spent training will be wasted. Training the mind is mastering your own mind-myth narrative. Consequently, we might say that when attempting to train the mind, you're not so much schooling it as writing the training manual.

All emotions are simply vaporous constructs of a mind subject to countless distractions. If you've not written your own narrative with intent, the distractions of life rather write themselves into the manual. The ideal situation is that these distractions are seen for what they are: either useful information or background noise in the music of life. Unfortunately, far too often these distractions overwhelm the mind. The mind then checks out, leaving control to its historical script, narrative, or program running on autopilot. True happiness, I suppose, is the ability to contemplate all information with a fair mind and productively edit your own mind-myth in a way that recognizes the underlying beauty of one's own life. This is the very definition of optimism. The thinker doesn't ignore that which is negative but seeks to put it in context.

Maintaining my own happiness has sometimes been a challenge. There is little doubt that a primary reason for this result has been my own quest for wealth and comfort. Though it has been difficult at times, ultra-thinking has allowed me to contextualize concepts of money. Issues related to personal finance or the economy may urge me toward positive or negative emotions; regardless, since these feelings are triggered by extraneous events largely beyond my control, I can usually isolate them from my person. I am not my own net worth or annual earnings. True, those things are important to me, but they are fleeting "things" having no real meaning in the existence of my person.

What I do is attempt to think of myself as two creatures. The individual "me" is that tangible body who earns, saves, and spends. The person "me" is my spiritual or meta presence. For this reason, I've often called myself a kind of dualist, though one who studies philosophy may disagree with my use of the term. When it comes to money, I feel its need is driven by the individual; therefore, though money is a meta concept, its practical use lies in the material realm. What this tells me is that money can be considered meaningless to my meta self. Since emotions like happiness are meta things, and money is irrelevant to my own meta self, I am at liberty to dismiss or elevate money ideas at my own whim. The individual needs money; the person does not.

Of course, all of these mind games are wonderful when they work, but sometimes they don't. When I lose my own game I'm as fearful, mad, and frustrated about money as anyone else. I can't always stay optimistic and isolate the negatives of life. In order to encourage my own attitude toward a more optimistic tone, years ago I adopted a sort of mental motto: Shoot for a grade of "A" but be happy with a "C" since it's a far better grade than an incomplete. As silly as this sounds, I've managed to live my life by this motto. For me, it helps lighten the stress of my mind. With my motto in mind, I seem to be better able to shrug off a subpar result. So, if you happen to rate my book a "two," oh well, at least I tried. I'm still happier for having written than not.

Obviously, with a motto like mine, I'm no perfectionist. I'm a manager-type who ascribes greater value to getting a task done than getting a task done with perfection. You think differently than I. You may be that ultimate perfectionist or procrastinating underachiever. It's all good my friend. We're all who we are, and those are some really cool beings in the cosmos. Once you understand the orientation of your mind and can notice reflexive thought patterns, those which push you toward unhappiness should certainly be well managed.

Negative emotions probably shouldn't be completely eliminated, but certainly, when they are the result of something so urbane as money, I doubt they offer many benefits to your cosmic existence. What does matter is taking time to understand who you are. Once you start to figure yourself out you'll be better equipped to make financial decisions which don't conflict with your fundamental style, attitude, and way of thought.

Relieving conflict and stress are critical to achieving a state of happiness.

Given the rather obvious fact that money heavily influences personal happiness, it is astounding that more people aren't willing to drill down into their own minds. People would benefit from better understanding the dynamic relationship between mind, money, and happiness. The myth promoted by society and adopted by most is that more money indirectly brings added happiness as a result of the pleasures it affords. Naturally, we'd then assume the converse is true; unhappiness is associated with little money. I'm telling you all of these ideas, myths, are just concepts. Internalize the truth of society or not. Either way, once you understand yourself you can acknowledge that your own truth is but a creation of intent or simple reflexive thought pattern.

Be a pauper or a billionaire, it makes no difference—you still have only one chance at happiness. You alone are in charge. In charge of your ideas, your predictions, your goals, and your personal finances. That is all you can truly control in the end. I suggest you conclude: happiness.

Now, get back to making money. Or … maybe you've got enough.

APPENDIX 1

# GET READY!

***What is the issue?*** A widespread power outage lasting more than three days, probably two weeks or more.

***What is the cause of the outage?*** A high-altitude Electromagnetic Pulse (EMP) wave or Coronal Mass Ejection (CME) from the sun.

***Why is an EMP/CME a grave concern today?*** 1) While the sun frequently emits these types of waves, we have not recently been in the path of these plasmatic/magnetic waves of highly charged particles. Although common, the waves from the sun tend to have a relatively narrow focus; therefore, our little planet hasn't been severely impacted by such an event since the modern age of an interconnected power grid and full reliance on satellite communications. 2) Over the past twenty years, techniques have been developed which can generate an EMP artificially. The use of a high-altitude nuclear explosion to produce an EMP wave as a weapon is becoming more likely according to informed sources.

***Is this really such a problem?*** Most modern electronic devices and, more importantly, the power grid would be severely impacted if in the path of an EMP/CME wave (event). On the other hand, this wave is harmless to our biology and that of other living organisms. But consider being without power and therefore *most* of our essentials of modern living for days, weeks, or months. You should know that should such an event occur it is likely your tap water will stop flowing within hours, and the stores will be closed. Things will get serious very quickly.

***What is the likelihood that within the next twenty years an event would happen that impacts the northern hemisphere of our planet?*** Experts say this is a near certainty.

***What is the chance that you personally will be affected by such an event?*** A 10% chance is a reasonable guess that over the next twenty years *you* would be affected.

***How would you know an event has happened?*** You're in a widespread power outage, and your cell phone is down as well for more than six hours without readily available information.

***What should you watch out for after an event?*** Misinformation may be the biggest problem. The more directly sourced information you have, the better off you'll be. Radio stations should be up and running first. You should expect lines for water, food, fuel, information, and congregating citizens at social service areas like hospitals and fire stations. Expect to see panic in the streets by day three or four. As power is restored, expect brownouts or rotating blackouts. Be prepared to give social agencies weeks to restore general order. Society could be impacted for years after a major event.

**Minimum Preparations**

1. A one-month supply of water (one gallon per day, per person, is a rough estimate of the absolute minimum necessary).

2. A two-week supply of food (think storable canned goods).

3. An AM/FM radio (EMP bag/box, see below) and batteries for a month or more. Regular batter-

ies need not be protected from an event, but rechargeable ones do.

4. A non-smartphone cell phone and charger (place in EMP bag). Although you may not have full service, the phone may prove valuable for 911 calls and/or post-event activation. Any phones not protected would have been fried, and if you can get this phone activated, you'd be in better shape than other people. Consider an unlocked 3G or older cell phone. The simpler the better.

5. A flashlight that uses the same batteries as your radio (place in EMP bag) and candles (matches).

6. You should keep some cash. (Remember, your cards won't work, the web is down, or data is suspect in general). There may not be much you can buy, but at least you'd have some cash should resources prove available. Expect a "bank run" should an event occur. Although you may have limited access to your bank money, in most cases, I would not be concerned that the FDIC would be in jeopardy.

7. A thumb drive or bigger device retaining critical personal, financial, and business data (place in EMP bag).

8. Think of what you'd need if you were camping for a couple of weeks, then create a list of items that you believe are personally critical for survival or leaving town on very short notice.

**See:**

http://science.nasa.gov/science-news/science-at-nasa/2014/23jul_superstorm/

http://thesurvivalmom.com/why-and-how-to-protect-your-gear-from-emp/ http://www.ready.gov/water

**Other Considerations**

Don't make it common knowledge that you are prepared. If you find yourself in an event, stand in a line on occasion just to look like another unprepared soul. Otherwise, you'll be supporting your friends and neighbors if they find out you're prepared to the slightest extent!

Old fashioned *postage stamps*. Mail a letter/note the day of an event to family/friends letting them know your plans. Believe it or not, the U.S. Postal Service will do everything in their power to clear the mail. Delivering mail will send a message to the public, and the Feds will want to give the appearance of order a.s.a.p. Create a written list of addresses and phone numbers of everyone important to you.

An extra tank or two of propane fuel for your grill (matches, lighters). A few extra gallons of gasoline for your car. (Safe storage is mandatory, and remember you must rotate a fresh supply every six months or so.) Some suggest you always keep a quarter tank of fuel in your car. Will your car work? Maybe, but what about that nice key fob?

A shovel.

Water, water, water! Your water heater stores some water; don't waste it. Remember, 1/8 teaspoon of bleach per gallon of water will somewhat disinfect drinking water provided it is not cloudy or muddy. Always let the water sit for thirty minutes before drinking disinfected water, and keep the bleached water out of the sun. Of course, boiling (two minutes at a rolling boil or three minutes at higher altitudes) works as well.

Batteries, batteries, batteries! A massive pack of name-brand batteries is available for $20. Provided you keep them fairly cool, they can last five or more years. Rechargeable batteries sound like a good idea, but they don't have the shelf life unless you cycle them at least annually.

Books to read, cards, board games, or something to entertain yourself.

A bicycle, significant bike lock, hand pump, and tire repair kit.

Personal toiletries and hand sanitizer (wipes, etc.).

Plastic trash bags.

"Blue ice" and a cooler (medicine storage). Remember, brownouts are likely.

A sixty-plus day supply of medication. Possibly consider radiation/iodine tablets.

First aid kit with a Z-Pak (or similar) set of antibiotics. (Include alcohol, peroxide, etc.)

A specific meeting or communication plan for family and friends. Consider agreeing to a specific plan to address the elderly, handicapped, and small children.

Build a Faraday cage for additional EMP/CME protected storage. (See below.)

A written list of critical addresses/phone numbers and numbers of bank, credit, and other financial accounts. Store a pdf file of statement copies on the thumb drive as well.

Personal protection. (Consider your actions at a time of civil unrest.)

Water filtration device and purification tabs.

A means of carrying water from a public access point: a hospital, for example.

Sunscreen lotion and other protection (shade canopy, sunscreen tarps, hats, etc.).

A basic tool kit. (Tie wire, rope, duct tape, etc.)

A landline telephone that operates without batteries (place in EMP Bag). Even if you don't have a landline, you may be able to find a point of access. When and if some service is restored, you'll be ready.

Secondary EMP bag. Yes, maybe this crosses the line toward paranoia. But it is an actual terror tactic to emit a minor EMP wave followed by a second larger event several days later. Your approach would be to use the first bag *only* to get information, wait a few days, then access the second bag when absolutely necessary.

Consider a relocation strategy *only if* medically necessary or the local issues are not likely to be resolved within sixty days. In short, force yourself to seriously consider locking up and moving on. Unfortunately, you will need to make this decision extremely early after the event. There is absolutely no way to evacuate major metropolitan areas quickly by car in case of an emergency, period! Your state and federal officials admit to this fact. So either you are first on the freeway, or you are stuck on the freeway. Once there are one or two accidents on any of the roads leading out of town, you will be camping on the road for days! Prepare for it.

A solar charging panel (place in EMP bag) and power bank (place in EMP bag) to charge the cell phone, radio, light, etc. You may consider having electronic devices that can be charged through a USB slot since these devices draw minimal power and might be charged via a solar panel.

*Side note:* A power bank (spare cell power devices) offers an efficient way to charge when used with a solar panel.

**EMP Bag**

If used properly an EMP Bag can insulate key electronics from an EMP and CME event.

1. After removing and setting aside any batteries, place your radio, phone, flashlight, thumb drive storage, and any other electronics in a box or bubble wrap envelope.
2. Place the box/envelope in a Mylar bag. The box/envelope insulates the items from having direct contact with the Mylar bag. Seal the bag.
3. Wrap the Mylar bag with at least 3 layers of heavy aluminum foil. The foil must be snugged up, sealing/crimping the foil seams as best you can. Seals and seams are critical; minor holes are less of an issue.
4. FYI: Batteries use a chemical reaction, so unless they're rechargeable, regular alkaline batteries themselves need not be placed in the bag.
5. Once you have your EMP bag wrapped in foil, simply place it under the bed or somewhere out of the way. Leave it! You are done.
6. To store many items, you may consider building a Faraday cage. A common method used to build a cage is to start with a 31-gallon metal trashcan. Again, you must protect your items from direct contact with the metal can. *You may wish to use a double trash can, placing a*

*smaller plastic trashcan inside the metal one, as this offers ideal insulation from direct metal contact, and it's easier than boxing the items.* Seal the lid of the metal can with reflective metal duct tape, and you are done. Theoretically, taping the lid is not necessary, but rarely does the trashcan lid seal all around the can tightly. The idea of the tape is primarily to push the lid down evenly around the can while reflecting waves away from getting concentrated under the lid. Grounding a cage is not necessary according to most sources. Others vehemently disagree, stating grounding is important.

7. You could create a small Faraday cage by putting items in a cardboard box. Then wrap the box with three to five layers of heavy foil.
8. A standard test of any EMP bag or cage is to place a working AM radio in the bag/cage with the volume turned up and properly tuned to a station. If once placed in the bag/cage you hear nothing, the protection is there. If you hear your station or radio static, you've failed and likely have cracks in the seams of your cage.
9. It should go without saying, don't run a power cord through to items in the bag/cage. The EMP/CME wave event is magnified by wires, since they serve as an antenna capturing the wave.

APPENDIX 2

# WORTHMIX CATEGORIES

**Cat 1: FDIC Cash**

FDIC cash is our first category. Don't confuse cash in hand with that categorized as FDIC cash. In this category I'm speaking of accounts not physical paper in hand. FDIC stands for the United States Federal Deposit Insurance Corporation. This corporation (company, insurance company) is a government-sanctioned entity that banks buy into in order to be licensed. Because this corporation's value is backed by the federal government in addition to the highest quality banks on the planet, the FDIC is often considered the single most stable corporation in the world as of this writing.

When I refer to "FDIC cash," this includes certain money market accounts, however, the term "money market account" is rather generic. All are not treated the same. Generally, money market mutual funds are not backed by the FDIC, and bank money market accounts are. See your bank for details, but normally the FDIC insures you personally against the loss of your money due to bank failure in an amount up to $250,000. Cashier's checks and money orders which have been issued by a failed bank are still insured. Safe deposit box contents, pensions, social security, annuities, etcetera, are not insured by the FDIC program.

A subset of this category is a Certificate of Deposit (CD). These are generally considered FDIC insured as are the vast majority of actual bank accounts. A CD provides an excellent way to fund Category 1. A CD usually pays interest at the highest rates offered by a bank, but the rates are specific to each deposit contract. The way a CD works is you commit money to the bank for a set number of days, months, or years. The bank pays you back what you committed, plus the interest at the end of the period. If for some reason you renege and want your money back—you cancel the CD—you typically forfeit all of the interest you would have gotten.

## Cat 2: Streams

People are confused by the term "bond" with respect to personal finance and certainly don't understand the nuance within various types of annuities; therefore, I call this category a "stream of money." Bonds pay interest, so they typically create a stream of income, and annuities act in a similar manner to bonds. Pension payments as well as social security payments are included in Category 2.

The reason people get confused with the word bond is that there are hundreds of varieties issued by hundreds of thousands of firms. So forget the technicalities and exotic types of bonds; when I say "bond" I'm speaking again of a rather plain vanilla version of bond. I'm simply speaking of a government- or corporate-issued bond document of high quality and a worthy mutual fund investment that holds the same types of bonds. Typically, you'd want the maturity on the bond to be no more than ten years. In a manner similar to a savings account or CD, bonds pay interest based on an interest rate. The actual receipt of the interest money may be delayed for years; however, the bond will ultimately pay you, the holder of the bond, some dollar amount of interest.

The word annuity is synonymous with the phrase "stream of money." If you purchase an annuity, you are buying a contract that promises to pay a stream of money. This stream is technically not interest. The stream of money you purchase is a mix of the return of the money you gave when you bought the stream and income on top of that amount. The total amount of payments received is calculated in a manner similar to interest, but because part of the stream is made up of your original purchase, it's not accurate to consider an annuity payment as interest income.

When the stream of money from an annuity is somehow related to retirement funds, it is often called a "pension." However, an annuity which is called a pension is not necessarily a formal pension contract. As is the case with so many financial terms, people use a catchall term which can mean many different things. A common difference between an annuity stream and a pension stream deals with insurance that the stream continues to flow as promised. True pensions are usually insured to a limited degree by the U.S. government. Annuities, even those called a pension, are not typically insured by the U.S. government. There could possibly be some type of insurance in guaranteeing the stream, but such insurance would not be from the federal government. That insurance probably comes from either the state that licensed the insurance company or a pool of other insurance companies.

In concept, annuities from insurance companies work as an alternative to social security or a formal pension. Annuities come in dozens of varieties, and some don't even require you to wait until retirement to turn on your money stream. Some pay death benefits, similar to life insurance. Any individual of legal age can purchase an annuity stream of money. That stream can be turned on immediately or in the future. That stream of money can pay monthly or annually for months, years, your lifetime, or you and your partner's lifetime. The bottom line is an annuity is a stream of money.

W. Durwood Johnson

Annuities in the United States are usually purchased over time by individuals through some type of retirement savings plan, however, they don't have to be. The value of that stream varies wildly depending on several factors—mainly how much money you want in the stream.

One of the unique aspects of the WorthMix model lies in how we treat your social security payments. Social security payments are an annuity (a stream of cash) that pays for your lifetime which does have a U.S. government guarantee. With this being the case, we assign it an asset value like any other pension. Using an assumed discount rate, one can value any annuity; therefore, you can assign a value to your social security stream just like you can a house, stock, or gold coin. A precise calculation relies on technicalities that are beyond the scope of this book, but we can get a ballpark figure with surprising ease.

I suggest you can get a pretty good estimation of the value of your specific social security contract through a rather basic calculation. Take your monthly payout times your realistic guess of life expectancy in terms of months. You may want to add or subtract between two and five years from the estimate depending upon your health, family history, or lifestyle. Multiply the number of months you're likely to live times the amount of the payment. Then cut the value by between 50% and 25% to account for the time value of money and likely impact of inflation on future purchasing power. The percentage discount increases with your assumption about the future rate of inflation. The product is a guesstimate of the value of your social security annuity. The figure for most of us will seem rather high, but I do believe the method provides a pretty good representation of the street value of the social security annuity contract.

As with any bond, annuity, or pension stream of cash, if you don't trust the contract cut the value you've calculated by some additional percentage. For instance, if I owned an annuity and the insurance company just filed for bankruptcy, personally, I'd consider cutting the expected value significantly. If I owned a particular bond issued by a corporation in or near bankruptcy, I'd cut the value by half or more. Theoretically, when you own a bond, annuity, or pension some trustee should give you something eventually, but that could take years.

### Cat 3: Stocks

Stock and stock mutual fund shares shouldn't intimidate you. For roughly the last eighty years, common folks like us have "been in the stock market." Some of us don't know how, why, or even what we're actually in; still, if you are a member of a 401(k) plan at work or own an IRA, you probably own stocks and/or stock mutual funds.

The value of a stock ultimately depends on what another buyer thinks it's worth. There is virtually no value of your stock in any company whatsoever if nobody wants to purchase it. Even if the company whose certificate you own has a billion dollars in cash in an FDIC bank account, even though you own a share of the company, *you* will never get a share of the bank account, period. The value of your shares is always determined by somebody other than you, and for most of us, it's the market that determines value in a stock.

Be advised that specific stock performance tends to have less to do with the finances of the actual firm than you'd think. Many "valuable" firms have gone under, and countless companies which have never shown a hint of profit sell for billions of dollars in the publicly traded markets. If the giant (broader) stock market goes down, then there is a very good chance the value of your specific stock will drop as well. True, some stocks move very little, some very much. Some stocks even tend to move against the tide, going up when the overall stock market is down and down when it's up. With that said, for the most part, publicly traded stocks of major companies tend to move in the general direction of the broader publicly traded stock market.

There are various ways to actually own stock, and we don't have time to go into all of them, but one of the most common ways to own stock is to own a "basket" of various stock certificates. Such a basket is one common way to refer to something called a stock or equity market mutual fund share. To be perfectly clear, when you own an equity-based mutual fund, you don't technically own the underlying stock. You own mutual fund shares in the broader pool. This is not necessarily better or worse, but you should be aware of the difference.

Mutual funds that most people own are managed by reputable managers or investment firm employees who do a very honorable job. I personally own both individual stocks and stock mutual funds. Funds are a more cost-effective way to own a basket of various stocks than for me to seek to fill my own unique basket. Managers I use follow the law and explain exactly what they have the right to do within the contract. Always read a mutual fund prospectus to understand your rights as a fund shareholder.

### Cat 4: Investment real estate

Real estate should be an easy phrase to understand, but it, like so many of these terms, can be confusing within the context of personal finance. Real estate in the United States is generally considered land plus what's attached to it. Land is a surface area of dirt from the center of the earth to the upper reaches of our atmosphere. The "plus" is anything affixed to the land in a permanent matter whether natural or artificial, with a handful of exceptions. Furthermore, there can be technical aspects to the definition of real estate as defined by cities, counties, and states. The main exceptions are airspace, crops, and valuable minerals including water. Semi-permanent structures like mobile homes and storage sheds are usually not treated as land because they're not considered permanently attached. Traditional homes, buildings, sidewalks, etcetera, are all considered real estate; they are the "plus" in "land plus."

Real estate equity is the value of the property minus the payoff of any loan or outstanding taxes on the property. Equity, or "net equity" in the context of this writing, means representation of net value. Net, of course, means one number minus another. So your equity in your real estate is its value (what it is worth in a fair sale) minus any loan secured by the property. Assume today your home would sell for $400,000 and the payoff on your mortgage is $245,000; you would then have $155,000 of equity in your home.

If you've been paying attention, you may notice I call this category "Investment Real Estate," not "real estate." I did this to exclude real estate that is considered a home or land which is so important to you that you'd never sell it. WorthMix is an investment model. Investments are not heirlooms, keepsakes, or things so important to you as to be priceless. Your home may fit in that category. If it does, your home is *not* investment real estate. In fact, its equity shouldn't be counted at all using my model. In my own case, I don't consider my home anything other than an investment asset, so I've included its value as being part of my own investment real estate in Cat 4.

## Cat 5: Hard assets

The dominant component of the hard asset category for most people should be gold and silver in my thinking. Here I'm speaking about a specific type of gold and silver. The type is actual physical coins issued by a reputable government mint, bullion. Austria, Australia, Canada, China, South America, and the United States are the most common producers of bullion coinage in the market. Bullion means a recognized government has certified the metals' weight and purity. Bullion can mean newly issued, older coins, and even bullion bars. However, be advised that many of the older coins are treated in the market as more of a collectible than bullion due to scarcity. Bars themselves are notoriously difficult to sell. For this reason, when I say bullion, I mean coins, new or older, but not of the collectible category.

Collectible numismatic gold and silver are certainly valuable; however, they are best left to the experts. Often when people discuss gold and silver they are speaking of a whole family of products: bullion, collectible coins, bars, slugs, stock certificates in mining companies, gold delivery receipts, contracts, exchange-traded funds, etc. I strongly suggest that you stick to bullion alone. The WorthMix model is a defensive model, so we want vanilla types of assets that are very likely to be marketable in most circumstances. Bullion will remain the most marketable type of gold and silver.

Gold and silver as financial assets are much more confusing than they should be. Keep it simple. If you seek to purchase bullion, make sure you establish a relationship with a reputable dealer; otherwise, you may be deceived. Even the experts can be duped, so relationship is everything. Therefore, it is suggested you seek bullion sold at gold spot market price, plus somewhere between ten and seventy dollars per coin for gold and two to five dollars premium per ounce coin for silver bullion. Yes, the premium does seem high and it can get extremely high when the coins are in great demand. For this reason, you should buy regularly and know your dealer. Dealers need to make some money, so don't expect them to sell you a bullion coin at zero premium. Just don't overpay.

The idea behind all investment assets is at some point you'll sell or barter them. You don't want to find out at the worst possible time that you have been defrauded or paid an unreasonable premium, meaning you won't make what you think you should when you sell. Be advised that when you sell back to a dealer you again pay a premium per coin. Consequently, a relationship with a dealer could be extremely important at some point, so treat them right.

Storage of something like gold, silver, and other Cat 5 assets is a challenge to put it mildly. Assuming the values of your hoard are meaningful, you'd want to use multiple locations for storage. Don't put all your valuables in one location. Wherever you put it, make sure someone in addition to you knows where it is and how to get it. I also urge you to use rather public locations for storage. Your home may sound like a good idea, and you may be tempted to use a home safe, but frankly, I think this could be the worst location to store very valuable hard assets. In times of distress, I wouldn't necessarily want a safe full of gold in the same home with my precious family. Furthermore, if you have a big safe, it's logical for an intruder to assume you have something important inside. I'd rather have it in, yes, even a bank safe deposit box than my closet. I know the risks. Certainly, if the power is out the bank won't have a way to let me get my stuff. This is why I say use multiple locations. Eventually, the bank will let you in, and they have security that you or I will never equal. Wherever you choose to store, do it.

Admit there is no ideal place, and don't fret too much. Pick a couple of places or even three, tell a trusted friend or family member, and get it done.

Collectibles as an asset can technically be about anything, even something like fossils. However, to be in my category, the collectibles need to be marketable. Even if it takes a while to sell them, they must actually be saleable in a reasonable period (say up to five years) to be considered of value. The market must be proven having lasted for more than twenty years. Vehicles, fine art (museum quality), rare books, and certain types of coins comprise the majority of collectibles. Don't be such a fan of your chosen collectible that you alone set the top of the market. Unfortunately, far too often collectors find they *are* the market. Finally, don't be misled by labels. Literally anything newly made and marketed as a collectible is not likely to ever be a collectible that you would consider an investment. With few exceptions, a newly made item that almost every buyer keeps in the packaging won't ever be worth much more than was originally paid for the item.

The biggest challenge with collectibles is marketability, sometimes called liquidity or convertibility to cash. This is why I consider them as a Cat 5 asset. Collectibles, done right, offer extreme diversification benefits. Furthermore, people can make crazy money on them if the investor knows the market. But, of course, those benefits come at a significant cost: time.

To get "fair value," let alone "top value," for a collectible is extremely difficult and time-consuming. Whatever price you've seen for a sale of a collectible, I say cut it by 75–80%; that's probably closer to what you could actually get for your collectible stash assuming you needed it sold within three to six months. If you have more time to sell, the closer to full value you're likely to receive. Therefore, cut your estimate of value by merely 50% if you have one year to sell, 25% for three years, and the cut in estimated value should be nil if you can market the collectible for five or more years. Like investment real estate, you should start marketing at least two, five, or even more years before you actually need the money.

Tradeables are the next subset of Cat 5. Tradeables are just as the name implies: something that can readily be traded or bartered such as fuel, water filtration equipment, ammunition, medical supplies, emergency equipment (solar generators), and other items. The typical survivalist stuff is what I mean by this term. I would not include food and water in the category unless you truly have access to huge quantities, say more than a one-year supply. You would not want to trade water for fuel unless you were sitting on an ocean of supply.

A further subcategory within Cat 5 would be physical money in hand. Yes, fiat paper money, and don't tell me that paper money isn't tradable. It is and will be until societal opinion fully abandons the idea; therefore, I suggest you keep some handy. Cash, including foreign currency, may prove invaluable. If you live near Canada or Mexico, having some of their money would probably be a prudent thing to do. No, I wouldn't go crazy with it, but in a worst-case scenario those foreign funds could be the only truly valuable currency. There is simply no way to predict. For most of us, cash means actual U.S. coins and dollars in a safe, or other secure and accessible storage location. Cash is not your credit card, your bank balance, debit card, or even your money market fund. I am literally referring to cash in the form of physical money.

Keep in mind that when the system is challenged, banks will impose a daily withdrawal limit of, say, $400. If the global banking Society for Worldwide Interbank Financial Telecommunication (SWIFT system) is hacked or somehow impinged, the banks will have no choice but to go into an account lockdown mode. The same with regards to your brokerage or stock account. The government, for a variety of reasons, often halts trading. When they halt trading, your funds are illiquid. Remember, even after 9/11, the New York Stock Exchange was closed for days. Some bank somewhere probably gets hacked every day, as do dozens of corporations including airlines and public works. You don't really think these multibillion-dollar companies have all of these "glitches," do you? Many of these so-called normal computer problems can be sourced to malicious actors who are out to mess with some corporation, government, or commoner. At some point, you and I will be impacted. Be prepared. Keep adequate cash on hand.

You need to have enough cash to cover your monthly cash outflow needs for at least six to twenty-four months. This recommendation is in addition to Cat 1, FDIC cash. I understand my recommendation of FDIC cash plus additional cash on hand seems rather extreme. However, you're reminded that any investment advisor worth her salt will tell you that you need to keep three to six months of cash in the bank. All I'm saying is double whatever safety net figure you'd typically keep on hand, and actually keep it in a bank safety deposit box which is readily accessible.

In the WorthMix model, I'm advocating a defensive investment asset allocation model and not trying to have you put your cash to work. I'm urging you to prepare for things like a bank run, financial market hack, significant financial market turmoil, or even a power outage that has financial implications. I go beyond common sense and recommend uncommon defense in tumultuous times.

# THE AUTHOR

The author, William Durwood Johnson, is a certified public accountant (CPA) currently licensed in the state of Arizona. Having been licensed for over three decades, he currently provides services on a regular basis to roughly four hundred clients ranging from engineering firms to wage earners. He's also a certified financial planner (CFP®), real estate agent, insurance agent, and stockbroker, though he does not currently practice in these fields.

Whether he simply snapped or made a rational decision is debatable; nevertheless, one day he decided to write and publish his own books in his spare time. He writes to advance his "Ultrathought" that when we work to identify and sequester our own ideological bias we can derive better ideas. Therein lies the key to creating an improved, fair-minded set of personal truths.

Durwood is one who actually believes we can succeed at whatever we try simply because we alone define victory or failure. Truth, life, and indeed one's very reality are but mind games played in the creation of self. Never forget that every single day on this planet a starving little girl has the best day of her life, while a wealthy heiress having the world at her fingertips cries out for death's release. The difference—mind. He suggests it's high time we ultra-think about it.

*www.ultrathoughts.com*
*ultrathoughtsbook@gmail.com*

www.ingramcontent.com/pod-product-compliance
Lightning Source LLC
Chambersburg PA
CBHW031349040426
42444CB00005B/243